DEV/12

D0489094

ALCOHOL AND H

A guide for health-care professionals

Marsha Y Morgan   **E Bruce Ritson**

2010

The Medical Council on Alcohol,
5 St Andrew's Place,
London NW1 4LB

Telephone: *0207 487 4445*
Fax: *0207 935 4479*
E-mail: *mca@medicouncilalcol.demon.co.uk*

REGISTERED
• 265242 •
CHARITY N°

ISBN 978-0-9563553-0-0

Published by The Medical Council on Alcohol,
5 St Andrew's Place,
London NW1 4LB

2010

Fourth edition 2003
Third edition 1998
Second edition 1986

British Library Cataloguing in Publication Data

Alcohol and Health: 5th ed.

I. Alcoholism. Medical and Psychological Aspects

I. Morgan MY
II. Medical Council on Alcohol

Design by the Medical Illustration Unit, Royal Free Campus,
UCL Medical School, London, NW3 2PF
Telephone: 0207 830 2357
www.ucl.ac.uk/medicalschool/msa/medical-illustration

PREFIX TO THE FIFTH EDITION

This book was originally intended for medical students and newly qualified doctors. These remain our priority but over the past decade many others who come into contact with individuals who are misusing alcohol, for example, nurses, occupational therapists, physiotherapists, alcohol counsellors and social workers, have found it useful. Thus, this fifth edition has been designed to further broaden its appeal, and extend its usefulness as a text for other health-care professionals, while not losing sight of our original remit. The text has been extensively revised with significant expansion of the sections on the predisposition to alcohol-related harm, the psychosocial aspects of problem drinking and the management of alcohol misuse. The chapter on the management of specific alcohol-related problems has been enhanced by the inclusion of illustrative case histories to deal with important aspects of commonly encountered problems for which there are no right or wrong answers.The importance of workplace alcohol policies is emphasised by the inclusion of a sample policy in the appendix which also houses a new section on alcohol and the law. The aim throughout has been to provide a comprehensive and pragmatic text which we hope will serve to interest, to educate and above all to help those who encounter and work with individuals with alcohol-related problems.

MYM and EBR

2010

The Authors

Marsha Y Morgan
MB ChB FRCP

Reader in Medicine and Honorary Consultant Physician
The Centre for Hepatology
Department of Medicine
Royal Free Campus
University College London Medical School
LONDON

E Bruce Ritson
MD FRCPsych FRCP(Ed)

Vice-President of the Medical Council on Alcohol
and
Former Senior Lecturer and Consultant Psychiatrist
Department of Psychiatry
The University of Edinburgh
Alcohol Problems Service
Royal Edinburgh Hospital
EDINBURGH

Acknowledgements

We are extremely grateful to Mimosa Healthcare, the Cheshire and Wirral Partnership NHS Foundation Trust and the Royal Free Hampstead NHS Trust for their financial contribution towards the production of this book.

We are also extremely grateful to the BMA Medical Students Welfare Committee for their contribution to the distribution costs of this book.

Several colleagues provided valuable contributions to the text including Dr Joan Trowell, Dr Anne McCune, Dr Guy Ratcliffe, Mr Tosh Owen and Mrs Katie Fay. Dr Thomas Wilhelm kindly provided the cerebral imaging.

We thank the patients who gave permission for their photographs to be published.

CONTENTS

The Medical Council on Alcoholism (MCA) was founded in 1967 by a group of doctors who were becoming increasingly concerned about the effects of alcohol on the health of the public. In 2001 the organisation changed its name to the Medical Council on Alcohol in order to more accurately reflect its role as a provider of information on all aspects of alcohol and health. The Council offers information and advice on a broad range of alcohol-related health issues to interested individuals, the media and the public at large. However, its prime aim is to ensure that medical students, in particular, and doctors in training, are made aware of the ways in which alcohol might impinge on their clinical practice. Increasingly, doctors are expected to take a lead in the identification of individuals at risk of developing alcohol-related harm and to play a significant role in their management. Many would argue, however, that the majority of doctors are inadequately trained for this task and do not receive sufficient support to undertake this role effectively. It is difficult to incorporate teaching on this topic into an already overburdened curriculum, despite its obvious importance. The purpose of this book is to 'fill this gap' and to provide information on alcohol use and misuse sufficient to meet the needs of medical students in training today and of their recently qualified colleagues. Doctors are not the only individuals who are called upon to play a role in the management of individuals with alcohol-related problems and it is hoped that this book will also appeal to others health-care professionals involved in this field.

Dr Guy Ratcliffe FRCP
Medical Director

GLOSSARY OF TERMS

Alcohol:
(synonym **ethanol**)

Ethyl alcohol

Alcohol conversions:

1 ml of pure ethanol = 798 mg ethanol
1 g ethanol = 21.7 mMol ethanol
To convert mg/100 ml to mMol/l multiply by 0. 217
To convert mMol/l to mg/100 ml divide by 0.217

Alcohol unit:

10 ml or 8 g of absolute alcohol, approximately (see text):

½ pint (284 ml) ordinary strength beer or lager
1 glass (125 ml) average strength wine
1 glass (50 ml) fortified wine, e.g. sherry
1 single measure (25 ml) spirits

Alcohol consumption:

Low risk
Intake unlikely to be associated with
the development of alcohol-related
harm if spread over 7 days

♂ ≤ 21 units/week
♀ ≤ 14 units/week

Hazardous drinking
Intake likely to increase the risk of
developing alcohol-related harm

♂ 22-50 units/week
♀ 15-35 units/week

Harmful drinking
(synonym: **alcohol misuse**)
A pattern of drinking associated with
the development of alcohol-related harm

♂ ≥ 50 units/week
♀ ≥ 35 units/week

Alcohol dependence:
(synonyms: **alcoholism, alcohol addiction**)

A syndrome characterized by the presence of three or more of the following:

- a strong desire or compulsion to drink
- difficulty in controlling the onset or termination of drinking or the levels of alcohol use
- a physiological withdrawal state on cessation of alcohol or its use to avoid withdrawal symptoms
- increasing tolerance to alcohol so that increased amounts are needed in order to achieve similar effects to those produced originally by smaller amounts
- progressive neglect of other interests
- persisting use of alcohol despite clear evidence and an awareness of the nature and extent of the harm it is causing.

Problem drinker:
(synonyms: **alcohol problems, alcoholic**)

An individual who is experiencing alcohol-related harm

CHAPTER 1

ALCOHOL, ITS METABOLISM AND CONSUMPTION

BEVERAGES AND THEIR ALCOHOL CONTENT

The alcohol content of the various alcoholic beverages differs widely. Thus, similar quantities of different beverages can contain markedly different quantities of alcohol. The alcohol content of a given beverage is, however, easily calculated from its percentage alcohol content by volume (% ABV), which is clearly marked on the container, multiplied by 0.78, the specific gravity of alcohol:

$$\% \text{ ABV} \times 0.78 = \text{g alcohol/100 ml}$$

The absolute amount of alcohol in a given drink can then be calculated by reference to its volume (Table 1.1).

In order to simplify the quantification and hence to facilitate assessment of alcohol intake, a system, based on defining quantities of beverages containing equivalent amounts of alcohol, has been devised for use in Great Britain.

A 'unit' of alcohol approximates to 10 ml or 8 g of absolute alcohol and is contained in:

- ½ pint (284 ml) of 3-4% beer, lager or cider
- a single small glass (125 ml) of average strength table wine
- a single glass (50 ml) of fortified wine, for example martini
- a single measure (25 ml) of spirits

This system is now widely used by the lay public, by 'alcohol agencies' and by physicians alike. As currently publicized, however, it is greatly over-simplified for a number of reasons:

- The alcohol content of beers and lagers varies considerably (Table 1.1), so that a pint of beer (568 ml) may contain from 2 to 5 units of alcohol, depending on its strength;
- Beers and lagers, particularly for off-licence consumption, are sold in cans and bottles, in volumes varying from 330 to 440 or 500 ml, which bear little relationship to the pint measure;
- There is no standardized measure for wine; a 'glass' may contain from 4 to 12 fluid ounces (114 to 342 ml) and so, depending on the alcohol content of the wine, from 0.6 to 4.5 units of alcohol;
- Measures of drinks consumed at home differ from 'standard' measures; beer is consumed from bottles and cans in varying volumes, wine measures tend to be larger while measures of spirits tend to exceed optic measures by a factor of 2.5 to 3.0.

The accuracy of the 'unit' system can be improved by taking differences in beverage strengths and volumes into account. The exact number of units of alcohol in a given beverage volume can be calculated from the % ABV using the information that 10 ml of absolute alcohol is equivalent to 1 unit of alcohol. Thus, the number of units of alcohol in a given volume of beverage equals:

$$\frac{\% \text{ ABV x volume (ml)}}{1000}$$

A half-litre can of 8% ABV lager contains 4 units of alcohol;

$\left(\dfrac{8 \times 500}{1000}\right)$

likewise, a 750 ml bottle of 13% ABV wine contains 9.8 units of alcohol.

$\left(\dfrac{13 \times 750}{1000}\right)$

(Table 1.1 and *Appendix A*).

A number of on-line websites are now available which allow accurate calculation of alcohol consumption, for example: http://units.nhs.uk/unitCalculator.html.

In recent years new ranges of 'designer drinks' have been marketed including fortified wines, such as MD 20/20 and Mad Dog, strong white ciders, such as Diamond White and Ice Dragon, fruit-flavoured lagers and ciders, such as Desperados and Maxblack, alcoholised soft drinks, the so-called 'Alcopops', such as Hooch alcoholic lemon, and fruit flavoured spirits-based drinks such as Smirnoff ice, Bacardi breezers and Archers.

The fortified wines have sweet fruit flavours such as cherry, banana and strawberry and a % ABV of between 13 and 21. The white ciders, which are filtered to remove colour and some flavours, have a % ABV of between

TABLE 1.1: The alcohol content of various beverages				
Beverage Type	Alcohol by Volume (%)	Alcohol content (g/100 ml)	Measure	Alcohol Content (units)
Beers/lagers/stouts/ciders:				
alcohol - free	< 0.05	0.04	440 ml Pint	0 0
low alcohol	0.5 - 1	0.4-0.9	440 ml Pint	0.2 - 0.5 0.3 - 0.7
standard strength	3.0 - 4.0	2.3-3.1	Pint	1.7 - 2.3
premium strength	5.0 - 6.0	3.9-4.7	440 ml Pint	2.2 - 2.6 2.8 - 3.4
super strength	8.0 - 11.0	6.2-8.6	440 ml	3.5 - 5.0
Designer drinks':				
'Alcopops'	5.0 - 6.0	3.9-16.4	330 ml	1.7 - 2.0
spirits - based	5.5		275 ml	1.5
cider - based	8.4		275 ml	2.3
wine - based	13 - 21		330 ml	4.3 - 6.9
Wines:	5.0 - 13.0	3.9-10.1	750 ml	4.0 - 10.0
Fortified wines:				
(sherry, vermouth, cinzano)	14.0 - 20.0	10.9-15.6	750 ml	10.5 - 15.0
Spirits:				
light (gin, vodka, white rum)	37.5	29.3	700 ml	26.3
dark (whisky, brandy, dark rum)	40.0	31.2	700 ml	28.0
Liqueurs:	14.0 - 40.0	10.9-31.2	700 ml	10.0 - 28.0

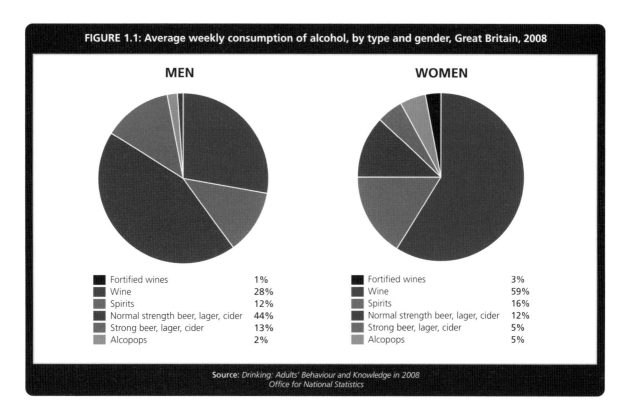

FIGURE 1.1: Average weekly consumption of alcohol, by type and gender, Great Britain, 2008

MEN

■ Fortified wines	1%
■ Wine	28%
■ Spirits	12%
■ Normal strength beer, lager, cider	44%
■ Strong beer, lager, cider	13%
■ Alcopops	2%

WOMEN

■ Fortified wines	3%
■ Wine	59%
■ Spirits	16%
■ Normal strength beer, lager, cider	12%
■ Strong beer, lager, cider	5%
■ Alcopops	5%

Source: *Drinking: Adults' Behaviour and Knowledge in 2008*
Office for National Statistics

8 and 9. The lagers and ciders, which are additionally flavoured with citrus fruits or blackcurrant and the 'Alcopops', which are essentially soft drinks that have been 'fortified' with alcohol, have a % ABV of between 5 and 6. The fruit-flavoured, spirits-based drinks, which are the latest addition to the 'designer range', are based on the so-called clean spirits, vodka, white rum and gin. They are flavoured with citrus fruits, although some have trendier, sophisticated flavours such as watermelon, cranberry and pineapple; they have an average % ABV of 5.5. All of these drinks are attractively packaged, often in small volumes, which may still contain several units of alcohol. The obvious appeal of these designer drinks to the younger, largely female end of the market is clearly a matter of concern (Figure 1.1).

The unit system is essentially parochial. Thus, in Australia and New Zealand, a 'standard' drink contains 13 ml or 10 g of absolute alcohol while in the United States of America, a 'standard' drink contains 15 ml or 12 g of absolute alcohol. Clearly this hampers international comparisons and makes assessment of epidemiological data extremely difficult (Table 1.2).

TABLE 1.2: International measures of alcoholic drinks

Country	Alcohol/drink
Great Britain (units)	10 ml: 8 g
Australia & New Zealand (drinks)	13 ml: 10 g
USA & Scandinavia (drinks)	15 ml: 12 g

ALCOHOL METABOLISM

Alcohol is rapidly absorbed from the upper gastro-intestinal tract. Approximately 80 to 90% is absorbed within 1 hour. The majority is oxidized, primarily in the liver; only 2 to 10% is eliminated in urine and breath. Hepatocytes contain three pathways for ethanol metabolism: the alcohol dehydrogenase (ADH) pathway in the cytosol; the microsomal ethanol oxidizing system (MEOS) located in the smooth endoplasmic reticulum and the catalase pathway located in peroxisomes (Figure 1.2).

ADH, which exists in multiple molecular forms, catalyses the conversion of ethanol to acetaldehyde. An 'atypical' ADH has been identified in between 5 to 20% of Europeans but in 90% of Mongoloid individuals. Although this isozyme shows a 7-fold increase in activity *in vitro*, its presence is not accompanied by an acceleration of ethanol metabolism *in vivo*. Gastric mucosa also contains ADH although a different isoform to those found in the liver. A proportion of ingested alcohol may, therefore, be metabolized in the stomach before reaching the portal system. The exact contribution, and hence the importance of gastric ethanol oxidation, is, however, debated.

MEOS activity has now been attributed to CYP2E1, an isoform of cytochrome P450. Its role in ethanol metabolism, in non-habitual drinkers, is probably small, at least when circulating ethanol concentrations are low.

Acetaldehyde is oxidized to acetate by the enzyme acetaldehyde dehydrogenase (ALDH). Two major isoforms of ALDH have been identified which play a major role in hepatic acetaldehyde metabolism; of these the mitochondrial form (ALDH2) is the more important. The ALDH2 gene is of considerable interest because it occurs in two polymorphic forms; the 'wild' type gene encodes the active enzyme whereas the 'mutant' form encodes an inactive enzyme. The mutant allele is rarely observed in Caucasians but is found in some 40% of Orientals; it is inherited as an autosomal dominant. Individuals carrying the mutant allele have a markedly reduced capacity to metabolize acetaldehyde and the resultant increase in circulating acetaldehyde concentrations produces general vasodilatation with a striking facial flushing response. The drug disulfiram (Antabuse) blocks the breakdown of acetaldehyde and the consequent flushing response is the basis of the Antabuse /alcohol reaction used as a deterrent to alcohol use. The acetate produced as a result of acetaldehyde oxidation is rapidly and safely metabolized to carbon dioxide and water.

Peak blood ethanol concentrations are attained approximately one hour after ingestion. A number of factors influence the levels attained, including the speed at which the beverage was drunk, whether it was consumed together with food, the rate of gastric emptying, and body habitus. Women attain consistently higher blood ethanol concentrations than men following a standard oral dose of ethanol (Figure 1.3). This occurs primarily because their body water, and hence the compartment in which the ethanol distributes, is

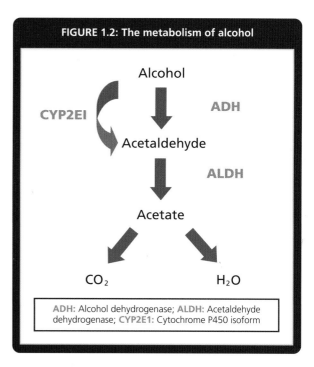

FIGURE 1.2: The metabolism of alcohol

ADH: Alcohol dehydrogenase; ALDH: Acetaldehyde dehydrogenase; CYP2E1: Cytochrome P450 isoform

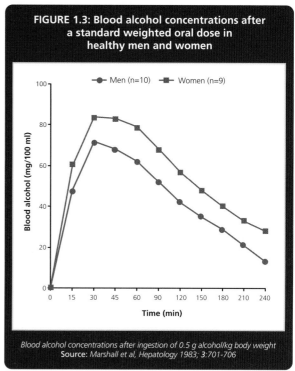

FIGURE 1.3: Blood alcohol concentrations after a standard weighted oral dose in healthy men and women

Blood alcohol concentrations after ingestion of 0.5 g alcohol/kg body weight
Source: *Marshall et al, Hepatology 1983; 3:701-706*

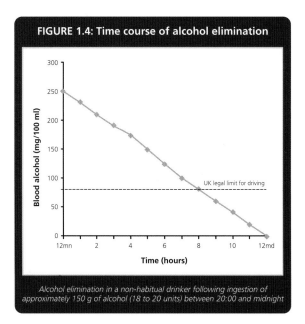

FIGURE 1.4: Time course of alcohol elimination

Blood alcohol (mg/100 ml)

UK legal limit for driving

Time (hours)

Alcohol elimination in a non-habitual drinker following ingestion of approximately 150 g of alcohol (18 to 20 units) between 20:00 and midnight

is, therefore, determined by the capacity of the liver to re-oxidize the NADH. Chronic alcohol misuse is associated with an increase in the metabolic rate of ethanol as a result of induction of the MEOS system; under these circumstances this alternative pathway can account for up to 10% of overall ethanol oxidation.

The oxidation of ethanol generates an excess of hydrogen equivalents in the liver, primarily as NADH. If the ability of the hepatocyte to maintain redox homeostasis is overwhelmed, then a number of metabolic disturbances may arise including, hypo- or hyperglycaemia, lactic acidosis, ketoacidosis, hyper-uricaemia, abnormalities of hepatic lipid metabolism and alterations in the metabolism of galactose, corticosteroids, serotonin and other amines.

EFFECTS OF ACUTE ALCOHOL CONSUMPTION

The rate at which the blood ethanol level increases is in turn determined by factors such as the amount of alcohol taken, the time span over which it is drunk, the rate of gastric emptying, which will be affected by the presence of food and certain drugs, and the individual's body size, gender and possibly ethnicity. In non-habitual drinkers blood ethanol concentrations of between 30 to 70 mg/100 ml (6.5 to 15.2 mMol/l) can lead to definite impairment of cognitive function, motor co-ordination and sensory perception, while concentrations of 150 to 250 mg/100 ml (32.6 to 54.4 mMol/l) are generally associated with obvious intoxication (Table 1.3).

The blood alcohol concentration required to produce intoxication will depend on a number of factors including: the rate of increase in the blood level; the degree of tolerance acquired by previous regular consumption, and the simultaneous effects of other drugs. In the early stages of inebriation there is interplay between the personality of the individual and the environment in which they find themselves. A rapid rise in the blood ethanol concentration produces a greater degree of intoxication than a gradual rise to the same level. In congenial company the drinker is often elated, becomes more loquacious, and may lose some of their normal social inhibitions. Solitary drinking may lead to feelings of depression and social isolation.

significantly smaller than in men. It has also been suggested that differences in gastric ADH activity may play a role in determining the gender differences in ethanol metabolism. Gastric ADH activity, and hence the capacity for gastric ethanol metabolism, is alleged to be lower in women than men; thus, following a standard oral dose, more alcohol is presented to the liver for metabolism in women and hence higher systemic concentrations are attained. This is, however, a contentious area, as gastric ADH activity varies with age and is significantly decreased in heavy drinkers.

Ethanol is eliminated from the body at an hourly rate of 7 to 10 g. Blood ethanol concentrations may, therefore, remain elevated for considerable periods following ingestion. Thus, if an individual imbibes 6 pints of premium strength beer (18 units) during an evening, their blood alcohol at midnight is likely to exceed 250 mg/100 ml (110 mMol/l) and will still exceed 80 mg/100 ml (35 mMol/l), the legal limit for driving, at 07:30 the following day (Figure 1.4); concentrations will be higher still in women drinking equivalently.

The rate-limiting factor in the metabolism of ethanol is the dissociation of the NADH-NAD enzyme complex. The ADH-mediated oxidation of ethanol results in transfer of hydrogen to the co-factor NAD converting it to its reduced form NADH. The rate of ethanol oxidation

With advancing intoxication the speech becomes slurred and unsteadiness and drowsiness develop, accompanied by autonomic effects such as flushing of the skin, dilatation of the pupils and tachycardia. At this stage reasoning and memory become increasingly impaired, perception is reduced, and the individual becomes readily distractible. Reduced motor and intellectual performance conflicts with feelings of enhanced ability. The individual loses emotional restraint and becomes excessively and sometimes inappropriately jocular, aggressive and occasionally paranoid or self-pitying.

More severe intoxication leads to increasing drowsiness and then coma, with depressed tendon reflexes, hypotension and hypothermia; respiration becomes shallow and stertorous. Death may result from respiratory depression or following inhalation of vomitus. The blood ethanol concentration at which death occurs varies considerably but concentrations of >450 mg/100 ml (98 mMol/l) are often fatal although survival has been recorded at concentrations ≥700 mg/100 ml (152.2 mMol/l) in habitual drinkers (Table 1.3).

Regular drinkers develop substantial tolerance to the intoxicating effects of alcohol so they need to drink more in order to achieve the desired effect. Habitual drinkers can, however, sustain blood ethanol concentrations of 300 mg/100 ml (65.2 mMol/l) or more without signs of intoxication.

RECOMMENDED DRINKING LEVELS

Alcohol taken in any amount may be harmful if the time and situation are inappropriate, for example, when driving. Indeed, the risk of sustaining alcohol-related injuries begins to increase with blood ethanol concentrations as low as 20 mg/100 ml (4.3 mMol/l). It is impossible, therefore, to

Amount imbibed (units)	Blood alcohol mg/100 ml (mMol/l)	Effects
2	30 (6.5)	Accident risk ↑
3	50 (10.9)	Mood ↑ ; judgement impaired; loss of inhibitions
5	80 (17.4)	Risk-taking behaviour ↑ ; jocularity; drink-drive limit
10	150 (32.6)	Loss of self-control; exuberance; slurring; quarrelsomeness
12	200 (43.5)	Staggering; diplopia; memory loss
25	400 (87.0)	Oblivion; sleepiness; coma
30	500 (108.7)	Death possible
38	600 (130.4)	Death certain

TABLE 1.3: The effects of increasing blood alcohol concentration in a näive male drinker

Blood alcohol levels are approximately one-third higher in women drinking the same amount of alcohol as a man of the same body weight, although in general women drink less than men.

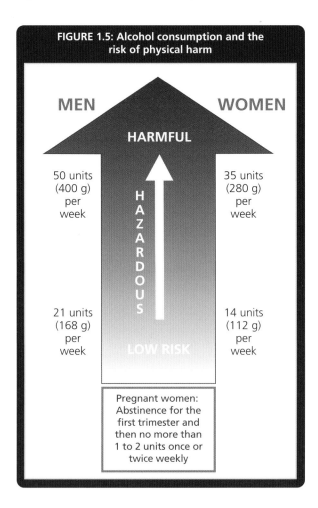

FIGURE 1.5: Alcohol consumption and the risk of physical harm

MEN — WOMEN

HARMFUL

HAZARDOUS

50 units (400 g) per week

35 units (280 g) per week

21 units (168 g) per week

14 units (112 g) per week

LOW RISK

Pregnant women: Abstinence for the first trimester and then no more than 1 to 2 units once or twice weekly identify a level of alcohol consumption that can be described as 'safe'. In the 1980s, however, the Royal Colleges of Psychiatrists, Physicians and General Practitioners sought to define more clearly the relationship between levels of alcohol consumption and the development of alcohol-related physical harm, excluding injuries. The consensus opinion was that, in men, weekly intakes of alcohol of ≤ 21 units and, in women, of ≤ 14 units are associated with a 'low risk'. Weekly intakes of between 22 and 50 units in men and between 15 and 35 units in women, described as hazardous drinking, are associated with an 'intermediate risk', while weekly intakes of >50 units in men and of >35 units in women, described as harmful drinking or alcohol misuse, are associated with a 'high risk' (Table 1.4; Figure 1.5). The findings and recommendations were endorsed by the British Medical Association (BMA). The differences in threshold levels between men and women reflect the fact that blood ethanol concentrations in women, following a standard oral dose, are approximately one-third higher than in men. Intakes in pregnancy should be reduced; abstinence is recommended for the first 3 months, while intakes during the rest of the pregnancy should be limited to 2 to 4 units a week, at most.

In late 1995, the Government established an inter-departmental working group to review the scientific and medical evidence on the health effects of drinking alcohol.

Their report set benchmarks for sensible drinking based on daily rather than weekly limits. It stated that 'regular consumption of between 3 to 4 units of alcohol a day, by men of all ages, and of between 2 to 3 units a day, by women of all ages, will not accrue a significant health risk', whereas 'consistently drinking 4 or more units a day by men and 3 or more units a day by women is not advised because of the progressive risk it carries' (Table 1.4).

The recommendations of this report have been widely misinterpreted, fuelled largely by the media, as 'relaxing' or 're-setting' the limits for sensible drinking to 28 units a week for men (4 x 7) and 21 units a week for women (3 x 7). Many medical and alcohol agencies, although recognising the benefit of setting daily limits, were unhappy with these recommendations primarily because of the failure to stipulate the need for 2 to 3 drink-free days a week, but also because health risks are known to increase at these 'newly recommended' levels of intake. In view of this, there does not appear to be any reason, at present, to change the low-risk thresholds from those originally set by the three Royal Colleges and approved by the BMA. Indeed there is compelling new evidence from reanalyses of the epidemiological data for further reducing the sensible limits for drinking for individuals below the age of 45.

The availability of stronger beers and lagers has made it more difficult for individuals to be sure how many units of alcohol they are consuming. However, the inclusion of % ABV on beverage labels may allow a more accurate assessment (Table 1.5). The inclusion of information on unit content on beverages would be of equal or greater value.

Considerable difficult is encountered in translating these so called recommended drinking levels internationally. This is likely to cause considerable confusion for UK residents when drinking abroad (Table 1.6; Figure 1.6).

TABLE 1.4: Recommendations on sensible drinking	
The Royal Colleges and the BMA	**The Government**
• Men ≤ 21 units/week (*3 units /day: < 4 units/day*)	• Men 3 to 4 units/day (*21-28 units/week*)
• Women ≤ 14 units/week (*2 units/day: < 3 units/day*)	• Women 2 to 3 units/day (*14-21 units/week*)
• 2 to 3 drink-free days	
• Pregnancy: 1 to 2 units 1 to 2/week	• Pregnancy: 1 to 2 units 1 to 2/week

Source: *Royal College of Psychiatrists, 1986; Royal College of General Practitioners, 1986; Royal College of Physicians, 1987; Department of Health, 1995*

TABLE 1.5: The number of 440 ml cans of beers containing 14 and 21 units of alcohol			
Beverage	Alcohol by Volume %	Number of 440 ml cans	
		14 units	21 units
Standard	3.6	9	14
Premium	5.0	6	9
Super	9.0	3.5	5

TABLE 1.6: International comparison of drink sizes and alcohol equivalents

Country	Drink size/alcohol content	Women (drinks/week)	Men (drinks/week)
Great Britain (units)	10 ml: 8 g	14	21
Australia & New Zealand (drinks)	13 ml: 10 g	11	17
USA & Scandinavia (drinks)	15 ml: 12 g	9	14

Based on intake of maximum recommended weekly amounts using the UK unit system

FIGURE 1.6: International comparison of drink sizes and alcohol equivalents

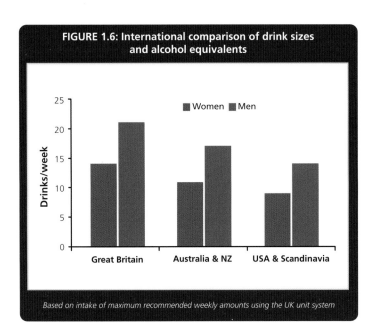

Based on intake of maximum recommended weekly amounts using the UK unit system

LEARNING POINTS

- Different beverages contain different concentrations of alcohol.

- Beverage content is assessed using the unit system.

  One unit (8 g of alcohol) is contained in:

  - ½ pint (284 ml) of 3 to 4% beer, lager or cider

  - a single small glass (125 ml) of average strength table wine,

  - a single glass (50 ml) of fortified wine, for example martini, or

  - a single measure (25 ml) of spirits

- The unit system is imperfect and should be used with caution.

- Alcohol is metabolized by the liver at a fixed rate of 1 unit/hr.

- It may take 12 hours for alcohol to be completely eliminated.

- Women achieve higher blood alcohol level than men of the same weigh because their body water is smaller.

- Intakes of alcohol should be restricted to a weekly total of ≤ 14 units for women and ≤ 21 units for men; pregnant women are advised not to drink in the first trimester and to minimise their intake thereafter.

CHAPTER 2

PREDISPOSITION TO PROBLEM DRINKING AND ALCOHOL-RELATED HARM

The majority of individuals drink alcohol in moderation throughout their lives, although some may drink above recommended levels at various times. A substantial minority of individuals drink at hazardous levels while some drink at harmful levels and may ultimately become dependent on alcohol. However, not all individuals drinking hazardously will go on to drink harmfully and not all those drinking harmfully will become dependent on alcohol. Likewise, a percentage of individuals drinking at hazardous and harmful levels will develop alcohol-related physical harm, perhaps systemic hypertension, cirrhosis or pancreatitis, but certainly not all.

The factors which determine an individual's propensity to drink harmfully and to become dependent on alcohol are largely unknown. However, environmental, constitutional and genetic influences are all thought to be important. Likewise, the factors which determine an individual's susceptibility to develop alcohol-related physical harm have not been clearly delineated. Again it is likely that environmental, constitutional and genetic factors are involved although these are likely to be distinct from the factors that determine drinking behaviour.

The various influences associated with the propensity to drink harmfully and to develop dependence on alcohol, and their interplay, can best be described using the classical medical model: agent (alcohol), host (individual) and environment. A similar model can be used to examine the factors associated with the susceptibility to develop alcohol-related physical harm.

HARMFUL DRINKING AND DEPENDENCE

ALCOHOL: THE AGENT

Men consuming alcohol in excess of 50 units/week and women consuming alcohol in excess of 35 units/week are classified as drinking harmfully. There is no evidence that the propensity to drink at these levels is influenced by the type of beverage consumed. Approximately 40% of these individuals will eventually become dependent on alcohol. There is no evidence that the propensity to develop alcohol dependence is influenced by either the amount of alcohol consumed, above the levels used to define harmful consumption, or the beverage type, although the risk of becoming dependent on alcohol rises with increased and more prolonged consumption. Individuals may change to beverages with a higher alcohol content as their drinking career progresses or may change to cheaper beverages if financial circumstances dictate.

INDIVIDUAL: THE HOST

Several factors may influence the predilection to drink at harmful levels.

Personality:
There is no evidence to support the belief that there is a typical addictive personality. Certain traits, particularly associated with anti-social personality disorder, are conspicuously common in the life histories of patients with alcohol problems but are more likely to be a consequence of years of excessive drinking rather than a cause. Evidence suggests that

younger male problem drinkers are more likely to have severe personality disturbances; they may drink excessively as a means of holding on to a precariously-held image of masculinity, and may have fathers who were themselves delinquent or problem drinkers. Individuals who are anxious, including those with phobic anxiety states, appear particularly vulnerable to alcohol misuse, and the association between depressive states, particularly in women, and alcohol dependence has long been recognized. Individuals with a psychopathic personality, characterized by impulsiveness, an inability to defer gratification and an inability to form close emotional ties, also appear to find alcohol rewarding and are immoderate in their drinking, as they are in many other aspects of their lives.

Inheritable Factors:

It is now generally accepted that 'alcoholism' runs in families. Indeed, it has been estimated that if an individual has an affected first degree relative then their risk of developing alcohol dependence is increased four-fold. Individuals with a positive family history, who themselves misuse alcohol, tend to drink earlier in life and to experience more alcohol-related problems than individuals without a family history. Twin and adoption studies have been used to assess the relative strengths of the genetic and environmental components of phenotypic variance. In the majority of twin studies greater concordance is observed for both drinking behaviour *per se* and problem drinking in monozygotic than dizygotic twins. Hereditability estimates of about 0.3 to 0.6 for the amount and frequency of alcohol consumption have been obtained by most investigators, where a factor of zero indicates no genetic influence and a factor of one indicates total genetic control. The results of twin studies do not completely exclude environmental effects. Identical twins may, for example, have a higher frequency of social contact than fraternal twins but when controls are exercised for this variable the higher concordance observed for drinking behaviour remains. Adoption studies can also be used to separate genetic and environmental factors in phenotypic variance. Such studies have shown that the frequency of alcohol dependence in later life is three to four times greater in adopted-away children who have at least one alcohol dependent biological parent.

Thus, twin, adoption and family hereditability studies indicate that genetic factors play a role in the predisposition to both drinking behaviour and alcohol dependence. However, a number of important questions remain, for example: (i) what are the heritable traits that influence susceptibility to harmful drinking and dependence? (ii) what are the genes that control the traits?

It is highly unlikely that the inheritance of harmful drinking and alcohol dependence is simply controlled. It is more likely to be polygenic and complex as it probably involves transmission of one or more intermediate characteristics or endophenotypes which subsequently affect the risk for harmful drinking and dependence (Figure 2.1). Each of these endophenotypes is likely to reflect the actions of multiple genes and to reflect both genetic and environmental influences.

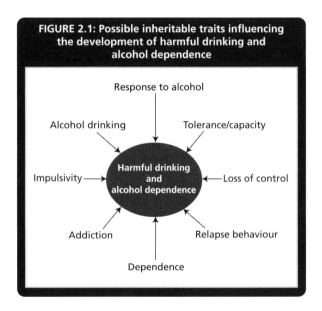

FIGURE 2.1: Possible inheritable traits influencing the development of harmful drinking and alcohol dependence

Genetic and associational studies have highlighted a wide range of genes which impact on diverse brain systems which may be of relevance to the development of alcohol use disorders. Some of these, such as polymorphisms of the GABRA2 gene, which is associated with impulsivity, disinhibition and other associated characteristics, and polymorphisms of various dopamine receptor genes, which are involved in reward and reinforcement, are potentially linked to the risk for both alcohol and illegal drug dependence. A number of other genes have been identified which are associated with a more specific risk for developing alcohol dependence but few of these have been replicated in later studies. The results of genome wide scanning might identify more specific targets for future study.

An ability to identify individuals genetically predisposed to alcohol problems raises the possibility of targeting educational and preventive approaches. The ethical dilemmas posed by such information require careful consideration. However, genetic studies may help to differentiate subtypes of problem drinkers who respond differently to treatment and hence may have different outcomes. For example, some subtypes may respond better to specific drug treatments than others, perhaps reflecting differences in the neurochemical responses to alcohol misuse.

THE ENVIRONMENT

A variety of environmental factors impinge on the individual and influence their consumption of alcohol. These include the prevailing climate of expectations, traditions and customs and the availability of alcoholic beverages.

Ethnicity, Culture and Religion:

Ethnicity and religion both influence alcohol consumption. However, a number of confounding social factors may influence the consumption patterns of individuals leaving the true magnitude of the link between religion, ethnicity and drinking behaviour unclear. In addition it may be difficult to distinguish between drinking patterns influenced by cultural practices and those which merely reflect the individual's socioeconomic/financial situation.

Migration and integration of populations is invariably associated with modulation and change in behaviours which have their roots in cultural and religious traditions. Thus, while cultural practices are likely to exert a prominent influence on drinking behaviour amongst first generation migrants, their influence is likely to wane in subsequent generations. Thus, drinking behaviour in young people from minority ethnic backgrounds, in the UK, is influenced by their social networks and peer behaviour. As a result, individuals who have friends from outside their own ethnic communities and/or own-ethnicity friends who drink alcohol are more likely to drink themselves.

Ethnicity: South Asians living in the UK, which in this context includes individuals originating from India, Pakistan, Bangladesh, Nepal and Sri Lanka, tend to drink less than the general population. However, south Asian migrants drink more than the native populations in their countries of origin. Hospital admission rates for

alcohol-related problems have shown a greater increase for Indian-born men in the UK than for the general population and alcohol-related morbidity rates for some south Asian communities are also higher.

Average alcohol consumption among the African/Afro-Caribbean population in the UK is lower than in the general population. Rates of heavy drinking and of alcohol-related problems are also about 50% lower in Afro-Caribbean men and women than in the native British population, findings which are consistent with those in African Americans.

The Irish are intensely ambivalent about alcohol and combine a high level of traditional condemnation of drinking and a high prevalence of abstainers with an acceptance and even a promotion of widespread alcohol use. Men from southern Ireland, living in the UK, have higher levels of alcohol consumption than the native population and much higher alcohol-related hospital admission and mortality rates.

Religion: There is considerable diversity in drinking practices between religious groups but simply holding religious beliefs can have an impact on alcohol consumption. Individuals with higher levels of religiosity, indicated by regular church/temple attendance and self-reported levels of the importance of religion, generally drink less. In particular, religiosity in adolescents has been shown to affect the formation of attitudes towards alcohol which may then persist into adulthood.

Islam, Hinduism and Sikhism promote abstinence. However, in practice it is only among Muslims that this precept is followed widely rather than being limited to the most devout. Nevertheless a small proportion of Muslims living in the UK report regular alcohol consumption and tend to drink more than the general population. This supports the belief that members of abstinent cultures who chose to drink are more likely to be disturbed and to drink abnormally; their drinking behaviour does not mirror their degree of religiosity. Sikhs are the heaviest drinkers both in India and in the UK where their consumption is nevertheless still lower than in the general population; however, heavy spirits drinking is increasing among Sikh men and is not confined to the younger generations.

Christianity and Judaism advise against excessive drinking and drunkenness but both use alcohol at religious events. Considerable variation is observed in

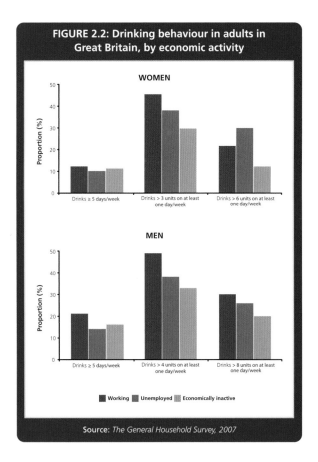

FIGURE 2.2: Drinking behaviour in adults in Great Britain, by economic activity

Source: *The General Household Survey, 2007*

FIGURE 2.3: Drinking behaviour in adults in Great Britain, by occupation

Source: *The General Household Survey, 2007*

drinking behaviour amongst Christian groups; the Pentecostal church, for example, strongly promotes abstinence while the Roman Catholic Church and the Church of England tend to adopt a more permissive approach. In the UK, and in the USA, Christians from African/Afro-Caribbean backgrounds tend to favour the Pentecostal movement while white Caucasians favour a more traditional approach. This provides a further example of how difficult it is to separate the relationships between religion, ethnicity and drinking.

Buddhism also promotes abstinence and the adherents in the UK, who are largely of Chinese origin, drink very little and considerably less than the general population.

Employment Status:

The data on drinking behaviour in relation to employment status reflect a number of confounding influences including income, financial commitments and free time; there are in

addition important gender differences. Thus, more employed men drink regularly and heavily than men who are either unemployed or economically inactive. However, in women, the heaviest drinking is observed amongst the unemployed (Figure 2.2).

Socioeconomic Status:

In general, men and women in the professional and managerial classes drink more regularly and are more likely to drink excessively than individuals in routine and manual employment (Figure 2.3). In recent years there has been convergence in the drinking behaviours of men and women particularly in the professional and managerial classes. This undoubtedly reflects the increased earning capacity of women in this group and the widespread acceptability of women drinking alone, or in groups, in bars and restaurants. This is clearly a worrying trend particularly when coupled with the fact that women are marrying later, a factor which has traditionally reduced overall levels of alcohol consumption in both women and men.

Parental Influence:

The double standard whereby parents and others in authority often endeavour to prohibit drinking amongst young people, while conveying by their own actions that it is acceptable 'adult' behaviour, only serves to make alcohol seem more attractive to young people as a means of marking their transition into adulthood.

Parents pass on their beliefs and attitudes to their children. These include their drinking habits and views about alcohol. Adolescents who grow up in a home where alcohol is assigned disproportionate significance are more likely to drink abnormally themselves. Paradoxically this pertains both when the parents are strongly 'anti-drink' and where one or both parents have a drinking problem. It seems that in such homes drinking becomes part of the emotional currency of the family. One consequence of this, coupled perhaps with a degree of biological vulnerability, is that alcohol addiction is four times more common among the sons of problem drinkers than in the general population. The family doctor is obviously particularly well placed to try and prevent the tragedy of alcohol misuse passing from one generation to the next by educating those at risk and by early detection of alcohol problems should they arise.

Peer Group Influences:

The peer group becomes increasingly important in adolescence and this can have a major effect on the pattern and quantity of alcohol consumed as well as beverage choice.

Availability:

Individuals in certain occupations may be at risk because they have easy, perhaps largely unsupervised access to alcohol. Equally it could be argued that individuals with a propensity to heavy drinking might seek out employment in environments where their drinking might go unnoticed or without comment, and might even be subsidized. It is not surprising, therefore, that publicans, bar staff, restaurant staff and brewery workers have higher than average alcohol-related mortality rates.

Cost is also very important. In relative terms alcohol has become cheaper in recent years. Between 1980 and 2008 the price of alcohol increased by 19% more than prices generally. However, households' disposable

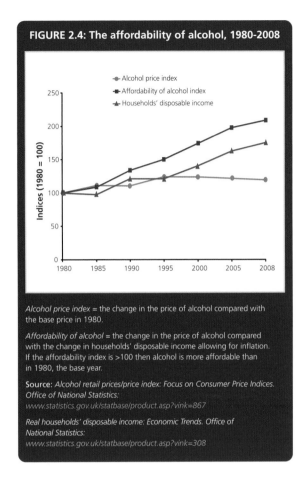

FIGURE 2.4: The affordability of alcohol, 1980-2008

- Alcohol price index
- Affordability of alcohol index
- Households' disposable income

Indices (1980 = 100)

Alcohol price index = the change in the price of alcohol compared with the base price in 1980.

Affordability of alcohol = the change in the price of alcohol compared with the change in households' disposable income allowing for inflation. If the affordability index is >100 then alcohol is more affordable than in 1980, the base year.

Source: *Alcohol retail prices/price index: Focus on Consumer Price Indices. Office of National Statistics:*
www.statistics.gov.uk/statbase/product.asp?vink=867

Real households' disposable income: Economic Trends. Office of National Statistics:
www.statistics.gov.uk/statbase/product.asp?vink=308

income increased over the same period by 109% making alcohol 75% more affordable in 2008 than in 2000 (Figure 2.4). In addition, many retail outlets, particularly supermarkets, reduce the costs of alcoholic beverages to levels that all but remove their profit margins. These 'loss leader' sales are compensated for by increases in the costs of other goods often purchased by customers attracted to the outlet by the lure of cheap alcohol. There is significant unrest about this practice.

SUMMARY

The predisposition to harmful drinking and alcohol dependence is thus multifactorial. A number of genetic, constitutional and environmental factors have been identified which undoubtedly influence drinking behaviour but it is likely that their relative influence will vary from indivual to individual.

ALCOHOL-RELATED PHYSICAL HARM

Considerably more is known about the factors that predispose to alcohol misuse and alcohol dependence than is known about the factors that predispose to the development of alcohol–related physical harm. Most is known about the possible factors governing the development of alcohol-related liver disease but there is some information on probable factors of importance in the development of alcohol-related pancreatitis, the Wernicke-Korsakov syndrome and alcohol-related malignancies.

ALCOHOL-RELATED LIVER DISEASE

Less than 20% of individuals who misuse alcohol will develop alcohol-related cirrhosis no matter how much they drink or for how long. The factors which determine an individual's susceptibility to develop significant liver injury are unknown. However, a number of variables which may be important have been identified (Figure 2.5).

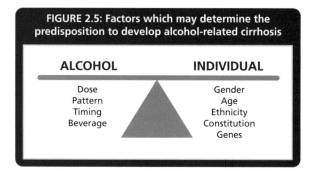

FIGURE 2.5: Factors which may determine the predisposition to develop alcohol-related cirrhosis

ALCOHOL	INDIVIDUAL
Dose	Gender
Pattern	Age
Timing	Ethnicity
Beverage	Constitution
	Genes

ALCOHOL: THE AGENT

The development of significant alcohol-related liver injury is associated with regular heavy drinking over a sustained period of time. Men drinking ≥ 40 g (≥ 5 units) and women drinking ≥ 20 g (≥ 2.5 units) of alcohol daily are at increased risk of developing alcohol-related cirrhosis. The risk increases with intakes of alcohol up to 60 g/day, in both men and women, but higher intakes are not associated with additional risk. There is little or no information on how long these intakes need to be sustained before the development of significant liver injury but the time-frame is probably much shorter than is generally perceived. Cirrhosis, once established, may not present for many years hence the misconception that it takes a prolonged period of time to develop. There is evidence that the risk of developing cirrhosis increases when alcohol is consumed outside of meal times and some evidence that the consumption of beer and spirits may be associated with a greater risk of developing significant liver injury than the consumption of wine.

INDIVIDUAL: THE HOST

A number of possible demographic, environmental and genetic factors may predispose to the development of alcohol-related cirrhosis.

Gender:

Women presenting with cirrhosis tend to have consumed less alcohol for a shorter period of time than their male counterparts. Hence, the widely held belief that women are more susceptible to alcohol than men in this regard. Women attain consistently higher blood alcohol concentrations following a standard oral dose (Figure 1.3). This occurs primarily because their body water, and hence the compartment in which the ethanol distributes, is significantly smaller than in men. However, although women may develop cirrhosis after lower cumulative ingestion of alcohol, there is no evidence that they develop liver injury after lower tissue exposure.

Age:

Individuals under the age of 35 years are at greater risk of dying as a consequence of drinking alcohol than all other age groups. Indeed, it has been suggested that the so-called sensible levels of consumption, currently recommended, are only appropriate for individuals aged 45 years or older. Lower levels are recommended for individuals aged 16 to 44 years (Table 2.1).

TABLE 2.1: Recommended limits of alcohol consumption, by age			
Men *(currently 21 units)*		**Women** *(currently 14 units)*	
Age (yr)	Limits (units/week)	Age (yr)	Limits (units/week)
16-34	7	16-44	7
35-44	14		
45-54	21	45-74	14
55-84	28	>75	21
>85	35		

*Source: White IR et al, BMJ 2002; **325**: 191-197*

Although the majority of deaths in the younger age groups relate to injuries a substantial numbers present with alcohol-related cirrhosis under the age of 30 years. Indeed, alcoholic liver disease ranks as the third commonest cause of alcohol-related deaths amongst 25 to 34-year-olds, after suicide and road traffic accidents, while it is the commonest alcohol-related cause of death in 35 to 44-year-olds.

Ethnicity:

Some ethnic groups may be more susceptible to the hepatotoxic effects of alcohol while others may be seemingly protected. Thus, Oriental individuals who carry the mutant ALDH2 gene have a markedly reduced capacity to metabolize acetaldehyde and the resultant increase in circulating acetaldehyde concentrations produces an unpleasant physical reaction which discourages further ingestion. Thus, they are 'protected' from developing significant alcohol-related liver disease because their intake tends to be limited.

In the USA the prevalence of cirrhosis is highest amongst African Americans and Hispanics but these are also the populations with the highest rates of poverty and social deprivation. In the UK, south Asian (non-Muslim) men are significantly over-represented amongst the cirrhotic population while Afro-Caribbean men are significantly under represented (Figure 2.6). Variations in body composition and in the metabolism of alcohol may explain these ethnic differences.

Constitutional:

Alcohol accelerates the liver injury associated with (i) obesity and the metabolic syndrome; (ii) toxin ingestion, including prescribed medication, over the counter medicines and herbal preparations; and (iii) hepatitis C infection. The liver injury which develops in these individuals is often wrongly ascribed to the effects of alcohol alone.

Genetic factors:

The concordance rate for alcohol-related cirrhosis is three times higher in monozygotic than dizygotic twins. The possibility that the predisposition to develop alcohol-related cirrhosis might be genetically mediated has, therefore, received considerable attention in recent years. A number of candidate genes have been proposed, including those that control the alcohol metabolizing enzymes *viz.* ADH, ALDH and CYP2E1, and those that relate to the various pathogenic processes thought to be important in the genesis of the cirrhotic process

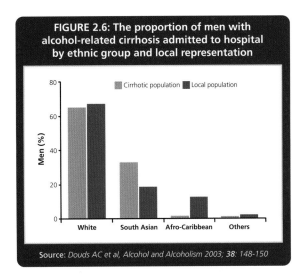

FIGURE 2.6: The proportion of men with alcohol-related cirrhosis admitted to hospital by ethnic group and local representation

Source: *Douds AC et al, Alcohol and Alcoholism 2003; **38**: 148-150*

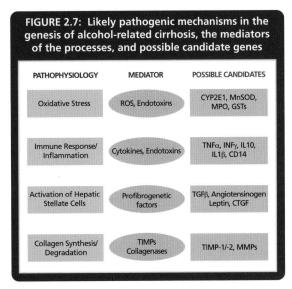

FIGURE 2.7: Likely pathogenic mechanisms in the genesis of alcohol-related cirrhosis, the mediators of the processes, and possible candidate genes

(Figure 2.7). To date, however, no replicated associations have been found. Nevertheless, this is clearly an important area for future research.

ALCOHOL-RELATED PANCREATITIS

The proportion of individuals who misuse alcohol and subsequently develop alcohol-related pancreatitis is unknown but is probably similar to the proportion that develops cirrhosis. No clear threshold dose has been identified; some individuals may develop this condition with alcohol intakes as low as 1 to 20 g/day (≤ 2 units);

others may need to drink in excess of 200 g/day (25 units) before evidence of the disease develops; others may never develop this condition no matter how much they drink or for how long. No specific associations have been identified between the risk of developing alcohol-related pancreatitis and the pattern or timing of drinking.

The propensity to develop alcohol-related pancreatitis may be due, in part, to additional environmental, constitutional and genetic influences. Amongst the best recognised of these are various dietary factors, hyperlipidaemia and smoking. Interest has also focused on the potential role of the genes that control the alcohol-metabolizing enzymes *viz.* ADH, ALDH and CYP2E1, and on the genes involved in the various pathogenic processes thought to be important in the genesis of chronic pancreatitis. Thus, associations have been reported with polymorphisms of the genes encoding carboxyl ester lipase, chymotrypsin C, cationic trypsin (PRSS1), the serine protease inhibitor (SPINK1) and the cystic fibrosis transmembrane conductance regulator (CFTR); however, few, if any of these associations have been replicated.

WERNICKE-KORSAKOV SYNDROME

Many individuals who misuse alcohol develop thiamine deficiency but only a very small proportion of these develop clinical features of the Wernicke–Korsakov syndrome. However, considerably more individuals show neuropathological evidence of the syndrome at post-mortem. It has long been suspected that genetic factors might play an important role in determining the susceptibility to develop this syndrome but no replicate associations have been found for the genes encoding for the alcohol-metabolizing enzymes, various thiamine dependent enzymes and certain GABA-receptors. Recently an association has been reported with polymorphisms in the high and low affinity thiamine transporters genes but further studies are needed.

ALCOHOL-RELATED MALIGNANCIES

Smoking is an important co-factor in the development of many of the malignancies that develop in individuals drinking at hazardous and harmful levels. There is also evidence that the risks for cancer development in individuals consuming excessive amounts of alcohol are modulated by genetic factors particularly polymorphisms in the genes involved in alcohol metabolism, folate metabolism and DNA repair.

LEARNING POINTS

Harmful drinking and dependence

- Intakes of alcohol of > 50 units/week in men and >35 units /week in women are considered harmful. Approximately 40% of individuals drinking at these levels will develop alcohol dependence.

- The factors which determine an individual's propensity to drink harmfully and to become dependent on alcohol are largely unknown.

- Although genetic factors are thought to influence both drinking behaviour and the development of dependence, the heritable traits and the genes that control them have not been identified.

- Environmental factors, such as ethnicity and religion, impact on drinking behaviour but are confounded by a number of social issues such as beverage availability, employment and socioeconomic status.

Alcohol-related physical harm

- Not everyone who drinks at harmful levels will develop alcohol-related physical harm.

- The factors that predispose to the development of alcohol-related damage vary in relation to the organ or system affected.

- Men drinking ≥40 g (≥5 units) and women drinking ≥ 20 g (≥ 2.5 units) of alcohol daily are at increased risk of developing cirrhosis but only 20% of harmful drinkers will develop this condition.

- Genetic factors most likely play a role in determining an individual's predisposition to develop cirrhosis but the heritable traits and the genes that control them have not been identified.

- Women, the young and south-Asian men appear to develop significant liver injury after lower alcohol exposure.

- Genetic factors, albeit not conclusively identified, appear to influence the propensity to develop alcohol-related pancreatitis, the Wernicke-Korsakov syndrome and alcohol-related malignancies.

CHAPTER 3

ALCOHOL-RELATED PHYSICAL HARM

The possibility that *acutely* intoxicated individuals may suffer abdominal discomfort and may injure themselves, intentionally or otherwise, is generally recognized; less well-recognized is the fact that they may develop gastrointestinal bleeding, cardiac arrhythmias, cerebrovascular accidents and respiratory depression, any of which may prove fatal. Equally, while it is generally acknowledged that individuals who *chronically* misuse alcohol may develop, and indeed die from cirrhosis of the liver, the fact that they may develop damage to every organ system in the body and that they are just as likely, if not more likely, to die as a result of suicide or injury, is generally not appreciated. Thus, while misuse of alcohol, whether acute and chronic, is associated with the development of physical disorders and harm (Table 3.1), the association between the two is often missed or ignored.

TABLE 3.1: The acute and chronic physical effects of alcohol misuse

Acute

Accidents and injury	Pancreatitis
Acute alcohol poisoning	Cardiac arrhythmias
Aspiration pneumonia	Cerebrovascular accidents
Oesophagitis	Neuropraxia
Mallory-Weiss syndrome	Myopathy/rhabdomyolysis
Gastritis	Hypoglycaemia

Chronic

Accidents and injury

Oesophagitis

Gastritis

Malabsorption

Malnutrition

Pancreatitis

Liver damage:
- Fatty change
- Hepatitis
- Cirrhosis

Systemic hypertension

Cardiomyopathy

Coronary heart disease

Cerebrovascular accidents

Brain damage:
- Dementia
- Wernicke-Korsakoff syndrome
- Cerebellar atrophy
- Marchiafava-Bignami syndrome
- Central pontine myelinolysis

Peripheral neuropathy

Myopathy

Osteoporosis

Skin disorders

Malignancies

Sexual dysfunction

Infertility

Foetal damage

These deleterious physical effects may be produced by alcohol *per se*, by its metabolites, or by the consequences of alcohol metabolism. Recent findings suggest roles in disease pathogenesis for gut-derived endotoxins, oxidative stress and immune responses.

Individuals' susceptibility to develop alcohol-related physical harm varies considerably (Table 3.2). Thus, for example, only between 10 and 20% of individuals who chronically misuse alcohol will eventually develop cirrhosis. The determinants of susceptibility have yet to be identified with certainty but genetic, constitutional and environmental factors are all likely to be important. Equally, habitual drinkers who have sustained alcohol-related harm may remain asymptomatic for long periods of time or else may present with florid symptoms and signs at an early stage. The factors which determine the 'degree of illness' associated with the development of alcohol-related organ damage are also largely unknown.

TABLE 3.2: The proportion of alcohol misusers at risk for developing selected alcohol-related problems	
Disorder	Percentage of alcohol misusers at risk
Cirrhosis	10-20%
Pancreatitis	15%
Cardiomyopathy	12-30%
Cerebral atrophy	60%

Alcohol-related physical harm is entirely preventable. Thus, every effort must be made to identity individuals at risk at an early stage. Once harm has developed it may still be reversed, to a large extent, by long-term abstinence from alcohol. Even individuals with established alcohol-related physical harm may benefit significantly, in terms of outcome, if they subsequently abstain from alcohol.

GENERAL FEATURES

Individuals who chronically misuse alcohol may develop a number of cutaneous and other superficial signs, irrespective of whether they have sustained major alcohol-related organ damage (Table 3.3; Plates 3.1–3.7). The mechanisms by which these develop are unknown, but, with the exception of Dupuytren's contractures, they may all regress, at least in part, following abstinence from alcohol.

Some of these signs may occur in association with other disorders; for example, spider naevi and palmar erythema may be observed in individuals with non-alcoholic liver disease, and Dupuytren's contractures may develop in individuals who sustain repeated, minor hand trauma. However, these signs, in constellation, occur most frequently in association with chronic alcohol misuse and, as such, are extremely useful diagnostic features.

A number of laboratory test abnormalities may occur in chronic alcohol misusers including elevation of serum aspartate aminotransferase (AST) and gamma glutamyl transpeptidase (GGT) activities and an increase in erythrocyte mean corpuscular volume (MCV). These abnormalities arise as a result of alcohol misuse *per se* and do not necessarily reflect the presence of significant alcohol-related organ damage.

TABLE 3.3: Cutaneous and other superficial signs suggestive of alcohol misuse
Spider naevi
Telangiectasia
Facial mooning
Parotid enlargement
Palmar erythema
Dupuytren's contracture
Gynaecomastia

Plate 3.1: Spider Naevi

Spider naevi are found only in the distribution of the superior vena cava, most commonly on the face and anterior chest wall. They comprise an enlarged central arteriole from which vessels radiate in a spoke-like manner.

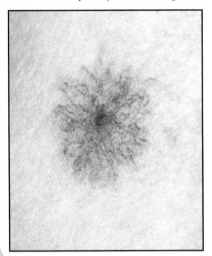 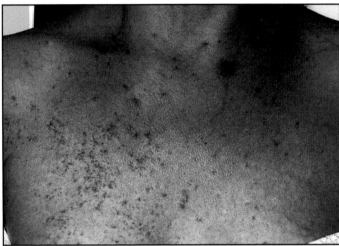

Plate 3.2: Telangiectasia

Linear **telangiectasia** or 'broken veins' occur commonly on the face giving it a 'weather-beaten' appearance.

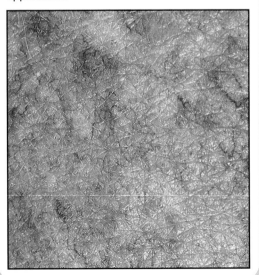

Plate 3.3: Facial Mooning

The face appears **rounded** or **moon-shaped**; the eye-lids may appear puffy.

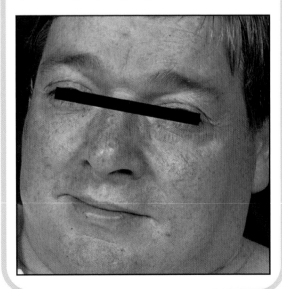

Plate 3.4: Parotid Hypertrophy

Parotid gland hypertrophy (arrowed) contributes to the rounded appearance of the face; the submandibular glands may also be enlarged.

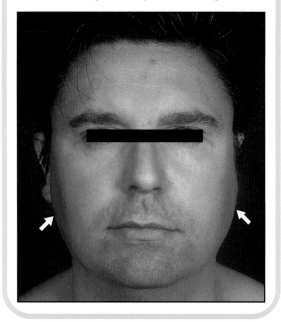

Plate 3.5: Palmar Erythema

Palmar erythema is characterized by a prominent rim of colour beginning on the hypothenar border of the hand but also, in some individuals, involving the thenar eminence and even the fingertips. Similar changes may be observed on the soles of the feet.

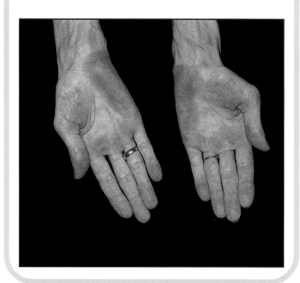

Plate 3.6: Dupuytren's Contractures

Dupuytren's contractures arise as a result of fibrous change in the palmar fascia which inserts into the flexor tendons in the palm of the hand; the ring fingers are most commonly affected. Similar changes may occur in the plantar fascia.

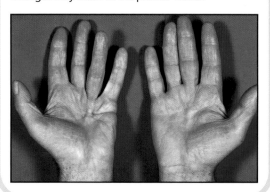

Plate 3.7: Gynaecomastia

Gynaecomastia or enlargement of breast tissue in men may occur either bilaterally or unilaterally.

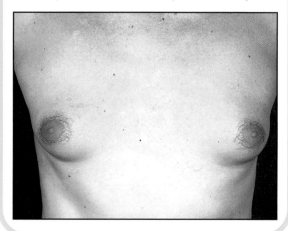

ACCIDENTS AND INJURY

Individuals drinking at hazardous and harmful levels, particularly adolescents and young adults, are at significant risk of sustaining accidental injuries. Indeed, accidental injury constitutes the largest public health problem in the UK today for individuals aged 1 to 40 years, and accounts for more deaths in adolescents than all other causes. Alcohol is a major factor in road traffic and other transport accidents, industrial and domestic accidents and accidental drownings and fire injuries. Alcohol is also a major factor in violent assault and homicide. Alcohol-related accidents and injuries are associated with greater morbidity and mortality than all other causes of alcohol-related physical damage (Figure 3.1).

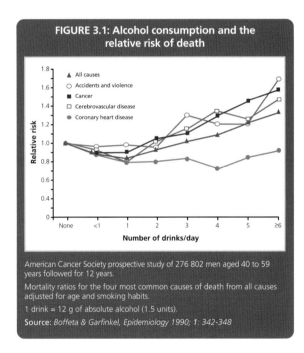

FIGURE 3.1: Alcohol consumption and the relative risk of death

American Cancer Society prospective study of 276 802 men aged 40 to 59 years followed for 12 years.

Mortality ratios for the four most common causes of death from all causes adjusted for age and smoking habits.

1 drink = 12 g of absolute alcohol (1.5 units).

Source: *Boffeta & Garfinkel, Epidemiology 1990; 1: 342-348*

GASTROINTESTINAL SYSTEM

Oesophagus:

The ingestion of large amounts of alcohol, over a relatively short period of time, may result in vomiting which can be violent. This may result in development of a Mallory-Weiss tear in the mucosa of the cardio-oesophageal junction, with resultant, often profuse gastrointestinal bleeding. Alcohol reduces the sphincter pressure at both ends of the oesophagus and impedes oesophageal peristalsis. In chronic alcohol misusers the resultant motor dysfunction may lead to the development of gastro-oesophageal reflux and, in consequence, oesophagitis, distal mucosal ulceration and Barrett's oesophagus – a premalignant condition in which the normal lining of the oesophagus is replaced by intestinal-type mucosa. There is a strong association between alcohol misuse and carcinoma of the oesophagus, particularly in heavy smokers.

Stomach:

Acute alcohol misuse may result in the development of acute gastritis; individuals may complain of nausea, vomiting and epigastric pain but the symptoms settle quickly after 48 to 72 hours abstinence from alcohol. Habitual drinking is associated with the development of chronic gastritis, which may be asymptomatic or else may be accompanied by a number of non-specific digestive symptoms. Chronic alcohol misuse is not, however, associated with an increased prevalence of peptic ulceration; indeed, alcohol misusers tend to have a lower prevalence of infection with *Helicobacter pylori* than non-habitual drinkers - alcohol might, in fact, have an important anti-*Helicobacter pylori* effect.

Small intestine:

Alcohol misuse, whether acute or chronic, is associated with the development of diarrhoea; this probably reflects changes in small intestinal permeability and motor activity. Habitual alcohol misuse is also associated with defective absorption of a number of nutrients including glucose, amino acids, vitamins and minerals, although clinically this seems to have little obvious consequence.

PANCREAS

Prolonged alcohol misuse can result in progressive and irreversible damage to the pancreas gland. This occurs on a background of pancreatic inflammation, acinar atrophy and, ultimately, fibrosis and can result in significant exocrine and endocrine insufficiency. Some individuals may develop this condition with alcohol intakes as low as 1 to 20 g/day (≤ 2 units); others may need to drink in excess of 200 g/day (25 units) before evidence of the disease develops; others may never develop this condition no matter how much they drink or for how long. In susceptible individuals the longer the duration of drinking the greater the risk of developing significant pathology. The propensity to develop alcohol-related pancreatitis may, at least in part, be due to genetic influences.

Alcohol-related pancreatitis is a disorder of men mainly in their 3rd to 5th decades. The stages and natural history of alcohol-related chronic pancreatitis have been difficult to characterize because patients may present with varying combinations of the main features. They may present with an acute episode of abdominal pain, nausea and vomiting and, in severe cases, with profound metabolic abnormalities and circulatory collapse. These acute episodes may recur, often precipitated by an increase in alcohol intake. Complications such as pressure on the common bile duct, localized leakage of pancreatic fluid and pancreatic exocrine and endocrine insufficiency may develop, resulting in jaundice, pseudocyst formation, malabsorption and diabetes. In some individuals, however, the clinical course is insidious with progression to pancreatic insufficiency without acute inflammatory episodes. Overall, however, the main clinical features of chronic pancreatitis are pain coupled with malabsorption/maldigestion and diabetes.

The diagnosis of alcohol-related pancreatitis is based on a history of alcohol misuse, suggestive clinical features, imaging to determine pancreatic structure, and assessments of pancreatic endocrine and exocrine function. A straight X-ray of the abdomen may reveal pancreatic calcification (Plate 3.8); abdominal computerized tomography (CT) scanning or magnetic resonance (MR) imaging may show evidence of calcification and gland distortion, while endoscopic retrograde cholangiopancreatography (ERCP) will identify the irregular and attenuated ductal system typical of this condition (Plate 3.9).

The most troublesome symptom is intermittent or continuous epigastric pain which may radiate to the back and flanks. The pain is usually managed with simple analgesics but the dosage and strength of these may need to be increased over time. Many patients require high dose opiates for effective pain relief. However, there are a number of interventional procedures which can be used to alleviate the pain if it becomes intractable, including: coeliac plexus block, splanchnicectomy, pancreatic endotherapy and surgery. Patients should be considered for these procedures at a relatively early stage. The exocrine insufficiency can be managed by use of oral pancreatic supplements, such as Creon, while the diabetes is managed conventionally with oral hypoglycaemic drugs or insulin.

Withdrawal of alcohol at an early stage may arrest the process and, even when the condition is established, may reduce the number of inflammatory episodes and allow for better control of both exocrine and endocrine insufficiency.

LIVER

Men drinking ≥ 40 g (≥ 5 units) and women drinking ≥ 20 g (≥ 2.5 units) of alcohol daily are at increased risk of developing alcohol-related liver disease. Alcohol produces a spectrum of liver injury but only a minority of individuals misusing alcohol, some 10 to 20%, develop cirrhosis; of these, approximately 15% will eventually develop hepatocellular carcinoma. The factors which determine an individual's susceptibility to develop significant alcohol-related liver injury are largely unknown although the amount, type and pattern of alcohol consumption are clearly important, as are the age, gender and ethnic origin of the individual, together with a number of, as yet incompletely understood, genetic, constitutional and environmental influences.

The majority of individuals who misuse alcohol will develop fatty change in their liver (Plate 3.10). Hepatic steatosis is an adaptive lesion, which arises because of changes in hepatic fat metabolism linked to the excess hydrogen ions generated during ethanol oxidation. Individuals generally present incidentally with non-specific gastrointestinal symptoms or else with complications of their underlying alcohol problems such as injuries or infections. The liver lesion is not in itself harmful and quickly reverses when alcohol is withdrawn. Only a minority of individuals with fatty change who continue to misuse alcohol will develop more serious liver injury.

Alcoholic hepatitis develops in probably less than 20% of individuals who chronically misuse alcohol (Plate 3.11). The majority may remain asymptomatic and escape detection unless they present for other reasons. A minority present with clear evidence of significant liver disease such as jaundice, poor clotting and fluid retention, together with evidence of systemic inflammation.

The outcome in individuals with alcoholic hepatitis is determined by their subsequent drinking behaviour, their gender and by the histological severity of the liver lesion. Thus, in men with mild to moderate alcoholic hepatitis, the liver injury is likely to resolve completely with abstinence from alcohol, whereas in women, and in individuals of both sexes with severe clinical, biochemical and histological disease, the liver lesion is likely to progress to cirrhosis, even with long-term abstinence from alcohol.

The mortality rate in individuals presenting with severe alcoholic hepatitis may be as high as 40%. However, the

Plate 3.8: Chronic Pancreatitis

Plain X-ray of the abdomen in a patient with **chronic alcoholic pancreatitis**; the calcification in the gland is clearly visible (arrowed).

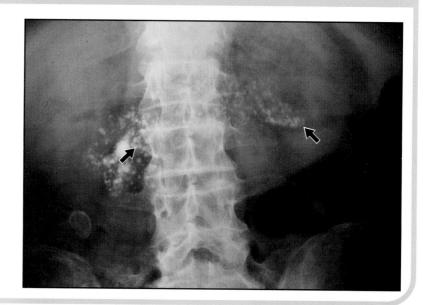

Plate 3.9: Chronic Pancreatitis

ERCP showing the appearance of a normal biliary and pancreatic system.

ERCP showing the appearance in a patient with chronic alcoholic pancreatitis; the pancreatic ducts are irregular and attenuated ; the biliary tree is dilated in this patient because of stricturing in the pancreatic head .

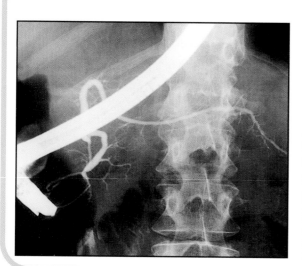

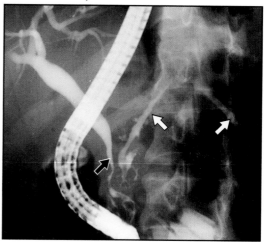

SPECTRUM OF ALCOHOL – RELATED LIVER INJURY

Plate 3.10: Fatty Change

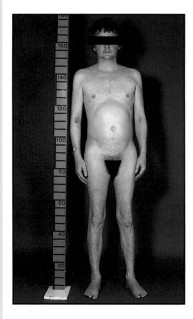

Patients with fatty change generally present incidentally either with non-specific digestive symptoms, or else as a problem drinker.

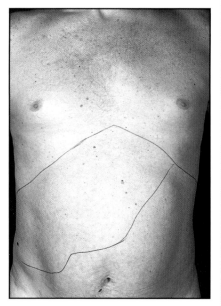

The liver may be significantly enlarged, as indicated, yet produce no symptoms.

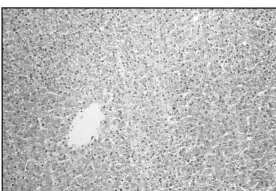

Normal liver:
H&E; magnification x100

Fatty liver: triglyceride is deposited in hepatocytes throughout the liver lobule.
H&E; magnification x 100

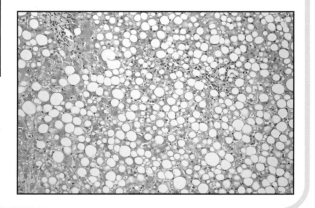

Plate 3.11: Alcoholic Hepatitis

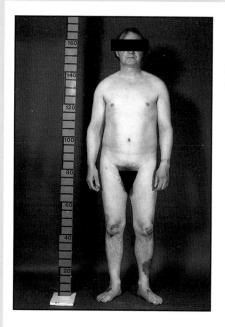

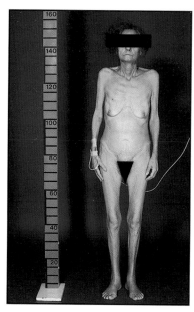

Patients may be asymptomatic

or present with features of chronic liver disease such as jaundice and malnutrition.

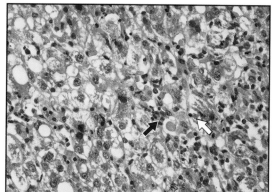

The liver architecture is preserved; the lesion is centrilobular and characterized by necrosis, inflammation ➤ and Mallory's hyaline ⇗ . H&E; magnification x 20

New collagen fibres develop around central veins ➤ and extend into the parenchyma ⇗ . Van Giesen; magnification x 400

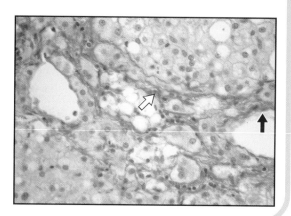

Plate 3.12: Alcoholic Cirrhosis

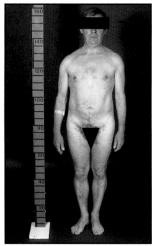

Patients may be asymptomatic

or present with features of hepatic decompensation including fluid retention, gastrointestinal bleeding and hepatic encephalopathy.

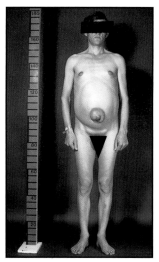

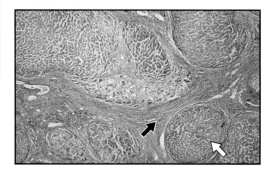

Micronodular cirrhosis:
the architecture is distorted by fibrous bands ➤ and nodule formation ⬦.
Trichrome; magnification x 20

Plate 3.13: Hepatocellular Carcinoma

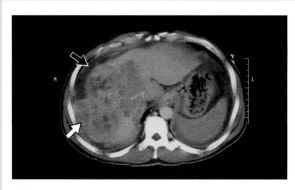

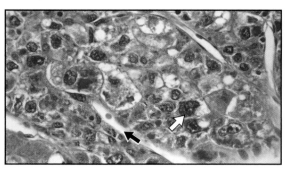

Abdominal CT scan in a patient with cirrhosis, indicated by the irregular liver margin and the presence of ascites ➤.   There is a large multifocal hepatocellular carcinoma within the hepatic parenchyma ⬦.

The tumour cells are smaller than normal with granular cytoplasm and hyperchromatic nuclei; mitoses are conspicuous ⬦; stroma is scanty and tumour cells have blood spaces between them ➤.
H&E; magnification x 600

outcome in these patients can be significantly improved by treatment with corticosteroids; typically 40 mg daily reducing over 6 weeks.

Individuals who develop alcohol-related cirrhosis may remain asymptomatic and come to attention only if inadvertently identified, for example, at an insurance medical examination; in these instances the liver disease is referred to as *compensated*. Alternatively, they may present with features of hepatocellular failure and portal hypertension, namely jaundice, fluid retention, blood clotting abnormalities, hepatic encephalopathy and variceal haemorrhage (Plate 3.12); the liver disease in these patients is referred to as *decompensated*.

The outcome for patients with alcohol-related cirrhosis is determined largely by the degree of decompensation at presentation and by their subsequent drinking behaviour. Thus, a middle-aged man who presents with compensated disease and subsequently abstains from alcohol has a 60 to 80% chance of being alive in 10 years, whereas a similar individual who presents with, for example, variceal bleeding, who survives the initial presentation but who continues to drink is unlikely to survive more than a year or two. The presence of superimposed alcoholic hepatitis and the development of hepatocellular carcinoma significantly reduce survival (Plate 3.13).

The most important management aim in patients with alcohol-related cirrhosis is to ensure long-term abstinence from alcohol. Complications such as fluid retention, hepatic encephalopathy and variceal bleeding are treated symptomatically. Orthotopic liver transplantation has a place in the management of patients with decompensated alcohol-related cirrhosis who have failed to improve despite well-documented abstinence from alcohol and expert medical treatment for a period of approximately 6 months. Survival rates are similar to those observed in patients transplanted for non-alcoholic cirrhosis. However, recidivism rates are still unacceptably high in some centres.

CARDIOVASCULAR SYSTEM

Both acute and chronic alcohol misuse can affect the cardiovascular system.

Electrophysiological Effects:

Acute alcohol ingestion may be associated with depression of left ventricular function and the development of ventricular premature beats even in individuals with 'healthy' hearts. More significant cardiac arrhythmia, such as atrial fibrillation, may develop after ingestion of more significant quantities of alcohol. These acute effects may be more pronounced and of greater clinical significance in individuals with pre-existing heart disease.

Blood Pressure:

Alcohol consumption is associated with increases in both systolic and diastolic blood pressure, which appear to be dose-related. Thus, systolic blood pressure is increased by, on average, 2.7 mmHg in individuals drinking 4 to 6 units of alcohol/day and by 4.6 mmHg in individuals drinking ≥7 units/day. These increases in blood pressure reverse when alcohol is withdrawn, at least in a percentage of individuals.

Heart Muscle:

Alcohol-related heart muscle disease or alcoholic cardiomyopathy develops in a proportion of individuals consuming in excess of 60 g (>7.5 units) of alcohol daily for a minimum of 10 years. Individuals with this condition may be asymptomatic and remain undetected unless discovered incidentally. Alternatively, they may present with non-specific manifestations of heart disease such as fatigue, palpitations or breathlessness, especially when the heart is stressed, or else may present with frank heart failure manifest as arrhythmias, raised central venous pressure, cardiomegaly, pulmonary and/or peripheral oedema.

The findings on ECG and chest X-ray are non-specific. However, echocardiography might identify and allow quantification of chamber dilatation and ventricular function. Confirmation of the diagnosis is obtained from cardiac catheterization studies and histological examination of cardiac muscle biopsies.

The cardiac changes in individuals in whom the disorder is subclinical will reverse entirely with subsequent abstinence from alcohol. Death occurs within 2 to 4 years of the onset of cardiac failure in individuals who continue to drink; the course of the illness may, however, be terminated at any stage by the onset of ventricular arrhythmias particularly in association with an acute episode of drinking.

The most important management aim is to secure life-long abstinence from alcohol. Symptomatic individuals are managed with diuretics and with antiarrhythmic agents, as indicated.

This form of low-output heart failure is quite distinct from the high-output heart failure observed, although rarely, in problem drinkers with thiamine deficiency; this so-called beriberi heart disease responds well to the prompt administration of high doses of thiamine.

Coronary Heart Disease:

Daily alcohol intakes of 1 to 3 units protect middle-aged men from coronary heart disease. Much less information is available in women, but daily intakes of 1 to 2 units may similarly protect those who are post-menopausal. The mechanism is uncertain although beneficial effects may include increased levels of high-density lipoprotein cholesterol, decreased levels of low-density lipoprotein cholesterol, prevention of clot formation, reduction in platelet aggregation, and lowering of plasma apolipoprotein(s) concentrations. Thus, alcohol reduces the risk of coronary vascular disease both by inhibiting the formation of atheroma and decreasing the rate of blood coagulation.

Cerebrovascular Disease:

Both acute and chronic alcohol misuse increase the risk of stroke; acute alcohol misuse possibly increases the risk of strokes overall whereas chronic alcohol misuse more especially increases the risk of haemorrhagic stroke. Alcohol also appears to be a risk factor for subarachnoid haemorrhage. Individuals who abuse alcohol are at increased risk of sustaining head injuries and hence of developing both subdural and extradural haematomata.

NERVOUS SYSTEM

Alcohol misuse can have profound effects on both the central and peripheral nervous systems; the damage may be caused either directly, or indirectly as a consequence of thiamine deficiency.

CENTRAL NERVOUS SYSTEM

A detailed discussion of alcohol intoxication and alcohol withdrawal is included in Chapter 7.

Chronic alcohol misuse is associated with the development of several organic brain syndromes. Although these are traditionally described as distinct entities, they may, and often do, co-exist. Individuals drinking at harmful levels are also prone to traumatic head injury and are at increased risk for recurrent injury. In consequence, it is not always possible to identify the aetiology of cognitive impairment, when it occurs, in patients with a history of chronic alcohol misuse.

Alcohol-related Dementia:

Specific cognitive deficits are demonstrable in some problem drinkers, which may or may not be accompanied by mild non-progressive impairment of intellectual capacity. Non-invasive neuroimaging shows evidence of cortical atrophy or shrinkage with reduction in the volume of the cerebral white matter (Plate 3.14). These changes in mental state and cerebral appearance reverse, to a variable degree, following prolonged abstinence from alcohol. The term 'alcoholic dementia' with its connotation of progression has been applied, somewhat unsatisfactorily, to this condition. More information on this topic is included in Chapter 4.

Wernicke-Korsakoff Syndrome:

The Wernicke-Korsakoff syndrome develops in problem drinkers who are thiamine deficient. However, thiamine deficiency is not invariably associated with the development of this syndrome so other, as yet unidentified factors, must also be important in its genesis. Genetic factors, perhaps relating to polymorphisms of certain thiamine transporter genes, may be an important predisposing factor in some individuals.

Wernicke's encephalopathy is an acute neuro-psychiatric condition characterized by global confusion, eye signs and ataxia; the confusional state is accompanied by apathy, disorientation and disturbed memory, but drowsiness and stupor are uncommon. The ocular abnormalities include nystagmus, gaze palsies and ophthalmoplegia, while the ataxia affects the trunk and lower extremities. The clinical abnormalities may develop acutely or evolve over several days. *Korsakoff's psychosis* is an amnesic state in which there is profound impairment of both retrograde and anterograde memory but relative preservation of other intellectual abilities in a setting of clear consciousness; confabulation may be a feature. Korsakoff's psychosis generally develops after an acute episode of Wernicke's encephalopathy. However, some patients develop a combined syndrome, from the outset, with memory loss, eye signs and unsteadiness but without confusion; others do not develop either the eye signs or ataxia. Less frequently the syndrome has a more insidious onset with either no documented history or only transient features of Wernicke's encephalopathy.

The syndrome is characterized, neuropathologically, by selective damage, including neuronal loss, in the paraventricular and periaquaductal grey matter; the subcortical areas thus affected include the thalamus and mammillary bodies along with the inferior colliculus in the midbrain and the vestibular nuclei and olivary complex in the brain stem. It is likely that damage to the mammillary bodies, the mammillo-thalamic tract and the anterior thalamus may be of greater importance in the development of memory dysfunction than damage to the medial dorsal nucleus of the thalamus. These patients may also show variable degrees of cortical atrophy, particularly in the frontal lobes, and cerebellar atrophy.

Treatment with high-dose parenteral thiamine should be instituted immediately the diagnosis is suspected (Table 3.4). Currently the only available preparation licensed for use in the UK is Pabrinex® which also contains a number of other B vitamins and ascorbic acid. This preparation can be given intravenously (IV) or intramuscally (IM); the IM route should NOT be used in patients with liver disease with defective blood clotting.

Wernicke's encephalopathy resolves rapidly following treatment but resolution of the Korsakoff's psychosis is less predictable. Approximately 25% make a very good recovery. Some residual memory deficit is observed in approximately 50% of individuals, although this can improve to a degree over time. However, in 25% the memory deficit remains severe and these individuals will invariably require some form of long-term institutional care.

It is clearly important to give thiamine prophylactically to all individuals consuming alcohol who are considered to be at risk for developing the Wernicke-Korsakoff syndrome. The dosage and route will be determined by the degree of perceived risk. It is not clear how long treatment should be continued to ensure adequate replenishment of thiamine stores – the figures given allow a safe margin (Table 3.5).

Cerebellar Atrophy:

A cerebellar syndrome characterized by varying degrees of ataxia, predominantly affecting the trunk and lower limbs, may be observed in harmful drinkers; the upper limbs are little affected and nystagmus and dysarthria are rare. Non-invasive neuroimaging shows atrophy of the cerebellar cortex mainly in the anterior and superior vermis (Plate 3.14). The condition improves following prolonged abstinence from alcohol but some degree of residual deficit is common.

Marchiafava-Bignami Syndrome:

This condition, which is characterized by demyelination of the corpus callosum, is rare. Affected individuals present with dementia, spasticity, dysarthria and an inability to walk; the clinical presentation may be acute, subacute or chronic. No treatment is available; patients may deteriorate very quickly, lapse into coma and die or else may survive, profoundly demented, for many years; occasional individuals recover completely after the acute event.

Central Pontine Myelinolysis:

This rare demyelinating disorder of the cerebral white matter is often rapidly fatal. It manifests clinically as progressive quadriplegia, pseudobulbar palsy and paresis or paralysis of horizontal eye movements. Its exact aetiology is unknown although its development is often associated with rapid correction of hyponatraemia or possibly other electrolyte abnormalities. Non-invasive neuroimaging shows a characteristic lesion in the mid pons which crosses the midline (Plate 3.15).

PERIPHERAL NERVOUS SYSTEM

Individual who misuse alcohol may develop focal peripheral nerve lesions as a result of compression injury when sleeping heavily or when stuporosed. 'Saturday night palsy' of the arm, which results from radial nerve compression, is the best example of this type of injury; recovery is invariably complete.

Alcohol misuse is the second most common cause of peripheral neuropathy in the western world, after diabetes mellitus. Prevalence rates of 30 to 70% are reported in unselected populations of individuals drinking harmfully;

symptoms and signs can develop after as little as one year of alcohol misuse. Both somatic and autonomic nerves can be affected. The commonest finding is of a symmetrical, bilateral, peripheral neuropathy, mainly affecting the legs. The symptoms are predominantly sensory and include numbness, painful cramps, burning and hyperaesthesia in a 'glove and stocking' distribution; motor features, include distal weakness, muscle loss and diminished or absent tendon reflexes. Involvement of the autonomic system is also common though often undiagnosed; symptoms including postural hypotension, changes in gastrointestinal transit time and erectile dysfunction.

The pathophysiology of alcohol-related peripheral neuropathy has been the subject of much debate; some attribute its development to the toxic effects of alcohol *per se* but others contend that factors such as thiamine deficiency and liver disease are of equal or greater importance. However, nerve biopsy studies have now shown that alcohol-related neuropathy is pathologically distinct from the neuropathy associated with these other conditions. Alcohol is likely to exert its direct toxic effect on peripheral nerves by interfering with the function of various ion channels.

Little is known about the natural history of alcohol-related peripheral neuropathy. Improvements have been reported in both autonomic and polyneuropathy following abstinence from alcohol but there is uncertainty about the completeness or the time scale of the nerve recovery. Abstinence from alcohol and supplementation with thiamine are the mainstays of treatment; muscle cramps respond well to amitriptyline.

SKELETAL MUSCLE

Skeletal muscle damage may develop in association with both acute and chronic alcohol misuse.

Acute Myopathy:

Acute alcoholic myopathy generally develops in association with an episode of acute intoxication or binge drinking. The spectrum of the disorder is wide; some individuals may be asymptomatic and are only detected because of elevation of their serum creatinine kinase activity, whilst others may develop an acute toxic rhabdomyolysis with myoglobinuria, acute renal tubular necrosis and fatal renal failure. The majority of individuals, however, present with some combination of: (i) myalgia or muscle pain, typically around the hip and shoulder girdles, and in the calves; (ii) muscle

Plate 3.14: Cerebral and Cerebellar Atrophy

Cerebral T₁-weighted coronal MRI scan in a healthy 58 year old women.

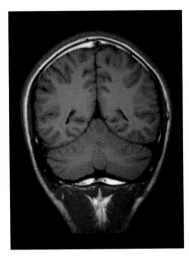

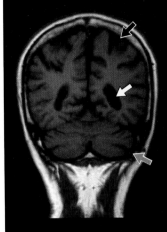

Cerebral T₁-weighted coronal MRI scan in a 52 year old women with a long history of alcohol misuse. There is evidence of cerebellar atrophy with prominent cerebellar fissures ↗ . There is also evidence of cerebral atrophy with prominent cerebral sulci ↗ and dilated venticles ↗ .

Plate 3.15: Central Pontine Myelinolysis

Cerebral T₂-weighted axial MRI scan in a healthy 45 year old man.

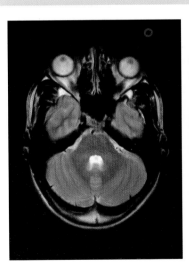

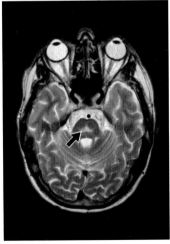

Cerebral T₂-weighted axial MRI scan in a 48 year old man with a history of chronic alcohol misuse. There is a patchy hyperintense lesion in the mid pons which crosses the midline ↗ characteristic of this condition. Cerebral atrophy is also present.

swelling and; (iii) progressive weakness particularly in the legs most noticeably on climbing stairs. Once alcohol is discontinued the symptoms resolve in days or weeks. Symptoms may recur after further episodes of heavy drinking.

Chronic Myopathy:

Individuals with a long history of chronic alcohol misuse may develop a skeletal myopathy characterized by selective atrophy of Type II fibres. Its prevalence is unknown as many patients may only have minor unattributable symptoms. However, up to 50% of harmful drinkers in some series have been shown to have some degree of muscle dysfunction. In general, alcoholic myopathy manifests as a progressive and usually painless wasting and weakness of the proximal limb muscles. Patients tend to complain of difficulty climbing stairs, rising from a squatting position, opening windows and combing their hair. The loss of musculature is associated with unsteadiness, frequent falls and osteopenia. The pathogenesis of alcoholic myopathy is uncertain although it is known to occur independently of the presence of malnutrition, peripheral neuropathy and liver disease.

Abstinence from alcohol results in considerable improvement in muscle function over a period of from 2 to 12 months. However improvement may continue for 3 to 5 years after cessation of alcohol.

BONE

Chronic alcohol misuse is associated with an increased incidence of trauma and injury, particularly bone fractures. Indeed, the term 'Battered Alcoholic Syndrome' was coined to describe the presence, on radiological screening, of multiple bone fractures, at different stages of healing.

Chronic alcohol misuse is also associated with an increased prevalence of osteoporosis and osteoporotic fractures. These individuals show a reduction in bone mass which is thought to reflect a direct effect of alcohol on bone remodelling and mineralization but other factors, such as nutritional deficiencies and cigarette smoking may also play a role. Abstinence from alcohol may result in some reversal of the process. Established osteoporosis is treated conventionally with calcium and vitamin D supplements, together with bisphosphonates, if indicated.

Individuals who misuse alcohol are also excessively prone to develop avascular necrosis of the hip for reasons that are unclear.

SKIN

Alcohol misuse is associated with the development of a number of cutaneous abnormalities such as spider naevi and linear telangiectasia, and is specifically associated with the development of discoid eczema and acne rosacea. Alcohol misuse can also precipitate the development of psoriasis in genetically predisposed individuals or else exacerbate existing lesions. In general the psoriatic lesions observed in alcohol misusers are more severe and more inflamed than in non-drinkers and occur in atypical flexural sites. Alcohol misuse is also associated with the development of seborrhoeic dermatitis and cutaneous bacterial and fungal infections. Abstinence from alcohol will help ameliorate these conditions or else render treatment more effective.

MALIGNANCIES

A causal link has been established between alcohol consumption and the development of cancers of the mouth, pharynx, larynx, oesophagus, colon and rectum and, in women, breast; an association is suspected, but not proven, for cancers of the pancreas, lung and kidney. The levels of alcohol consumption associated with the risk for development vary for each cancer. In some instances the excess risk is significant at relatively low levels of consumption. Thus, the magnitude of the excess risk of developing breast cancer is of the order of a 7% increase for every additional 10 g a day increase in alcohol consumption.

A clear synergism occurs between the risks associated with alcohol consumption and tobacco smoking in the development of cancers of the oral cavity, pharynx, larynx and oesophagus. Individuals with alcohol-related cirrhosis are at risk of developing hepatocellular carcinoma but alcohol misuse *per se* is not a risk factor for the development of this tumour.

The mechanisms by which alcohol exerts its carcinogenic effects are largely unknown and probably differ by target organ. Evidence favours a possible general damaging effect of acetaldehyde on DNA, the production of reactive oxygen and nitrogen species and a reduction in immune surveillance. Alcohol-related increases in oestrogen concentrations are thought to play a role in the development of breast cancer.

SEXUAL DYSFUNCTION AND INFERTILITY

Alcohol misuse may have significant effects on sexual function and reproductive capacity in both men and women. However, alcohol can have significant effects on fertility, even in moderate amounts, if taken on a regular basis. Thus, in susceptible men, alcohol intakes of 4 to 6 units/day can result in a significant reduction in the sperm count; in many such individuals abstinence from alcohol is associated with restoration of fertility. Women who drink more than 3 units/day may be subfertile; no information is available on the reversibility of this effect.

PREGNANCY AND FOETAL DAMAGE

Alcohol is known to be teratotoxic and foetotoxic when consumed during pregnancy. However, there is still debate about what constitutes safe limits of consumption. In some countries, for example Canada, pregnant women or women who are trying to conceive are advised not to drink alcohol at all. In 2007, the Department of Health in the UK recommended that pregnant women or women who are trying to conceive should avoid alcohol but if they chose to drink they should limit themselves to 1 to 2 units once or twice a week and should not get drunk. Clearly the question of what, if anything, is a safe level of alcohol consumption in pregnancy needs further debate.

Many women automatically modulate their alcohol intake on finding that they are pregnant. Indeed significant self-directed

TABLE 3.6: Features of the Fetal Alcohol Syndrome*

Pre- and post-natal growth retardation

CNS abnormalities including:
- Microcephaly
- Agenesis of the corpus callosum
- Cerebellar hypoplasia
- Mental retardation
- Irritability
- Hypotonia
- Inco-ordination
- Hyperactivity

Craniofacial abnormalities including:
- Short palpebral fissures,
- Epicanthic folds
- Smooth philtrum
- Thin upper lip
- Mid-facial hypoplasia
- Lower jaw hypoplasia
- Short upturned nose
- Minor ear abnormalities
- Ptosis
- Strabismus

Associated abnormalities including congenital defects of:
- Cardiovascular system
- Skeletal system
- Genitourinary tract
- Ocular system
- Auditory system
- Others

The terms 'Fetal Alcohol Syndrome' and 'Fetal Alcohol Spectrum Disorder' retain the American spelling of fetal as the term was first coined in the United States, although the features of the syndrome had been described earlier in France.

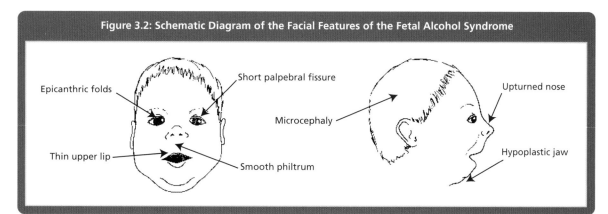

Figure 3.2: Schematic Diagram of the Facial Features of the Fetal Alcohol Syndrome

Epicanthric folds

Short palpebral fissure

Thin upper lip

Smooth philtrum

Microcephaly

Upturned nose

Hypoplastic jaw

reductions in alcohol consumption have been observed even in women formally drinking at hazardous levels.

Alcohol is an important risk factor for spontaneous abortion in the first and second trimesters. Thus, women drinking between 80 to 112 g (10 to 14 units) of alcohol per week have approximately four times the risk of a spontaneous abortion as women who are abstinent, while intakes of the same order at least double the risk of spontaneous abortion in the second trimester. Women who retain their pregnancies, but continue to drink, risk damaging their infants.

Regular consumption of alcohol, at any level, during pregnancy may potentially harm the foetus. The degree and nature of the abnormalities is determined by the amount and pattern of alcohol consumption and the timing of exposure in relation to foetal development. Other factors such as malnutrition and smoking may contribute to the damage incurred. The most vulnerable period is from 4 to 10 weeks gestation but alcohol-related damage may occur throughout the pregnancy. Thus, exposure during the first trimester can affect both organ and craniofacial development, while exposure in the third trimester has significant effects on growth.

The term Fetal Alcohol Syndrome Disorder (FASD) is used to describe the broad spectrum of abnormalities which can arise as a consequence of maternal drinking during pregnancy. These range from growth retardation to a constellation of abnormalities termed the Fetal Alcohol Syndrome (FAS) (Table 3.6; Figure 3.2). Only a small proportion of infants fulfil the diagnostic criteria for FAS. Others may have some of the characteristic features while others may have no outward abnormalities except for growth retardation. However, over time, these apparently unaffected infants may develop a wide range of mental and behavioural abnormalities including, attention deficits, problems with impulse control, aggression and other features of executive functioning, hyperactivity, inco-ordination and neuropsychological impairment. Considerable difficulty may arise in diagnosing FASD if the history of alcohol exposure during pregnancy is not available or else is denied.

FASD is the most common cause of developmental disability and of birth defects in the western world, and it is completely preventable. All pregnant women, and even those contemplating pregnancy, should be carefully questioned about their use of alcohol; the T-ACE questionnaire has been specifically designed for prenatal and antenatal screening (*Appendix B*). All women who are drinking alcohol should be provided with advice to stop and those who are drinking regularly should be referred for specialist assessment and help at the earliest opportunity. Alcohol damages the foetus throughout pregnancy so abstinence is likely to be beneficial no matter how late in the pregnancy the problem is uncovered.

LEARNING POINTS

- Individuals drinking alcohol at hazardous and harmful levels are at significant risk of sustaining injuries, which constitute the most important physical consequence of excess alcohol consumption.

- Acute alcohol ingestion, whether a binge or on a background of more sustained consumption, may be associated with the development of a number of physical problems some of which may end fatally.

- Hazardous and harmful drinking may be associated with the development of a wide range of chronic diseases or disorders affecting most organ systems in the body.

- The susceptibility of individuals to develop alcohol-related physical harm varies considerably; genetic, constitutional and environmental factors all play a role.

- The most important management goal in patients with alcohol-related physical harm is to ensure long-term abstinence from alcohol.

- Drinking during pregnancy is the most common cause of developmental disability and birth defects in the western world; no safe limit for alcohol consumption in pregnancy has been defined.

- All pregnant women should be routinely questioned about their alcohol consumption and advised accordingly.

CHAPTER 4

ALCOHOL-RELATED SOCIAL AND PSYCHOLOGICAL HARM

A number of social and psychological problems can arise as a consequence of both the acute and chronic effects of alcohol. Binge drinking, which has been a particular concern amongst young people, is associated with acute intoxication with its attendant risks of impaired judgement, impulsive behaviour, interpersonal problems, and accidents. Chronic alcohol misuse may be accompanied by a constellation of family, legal, occupational and psychological problems, which, if unchecked, might eventually lead to complete personal and social disintegration.

SOCIAL PROBLEMS

Social problems arise from an interaction between an individual and their surroundings. Their significance depends on the culture and context in which they occur. Drunkenness, for example, is more tolerated on some occasions than others. Indeed a high degree of tolerance or even an expectation of drunkenness is a feature of some occasions such as celebrations. Many of the social problems caused by acute alcohol intoxication, apart from those which put the individual at risk, arise when alcohol is consumed inappropriately such as when driving or looking after children. Chronic excessive drinking is associated with a number of major social issues such as divorce, unemployment and criminality.

It is hard to measure the exact extent of the social harm caused by alcohol. Statistics based on family breakdown, absenteeism and criminal offences represent only a small fraction of the day-to-day unhappiness and distress caused by alcohol and thus do not allow a full appreciation of the scale of the problem.

Social problems manifest in a number of different ways:

INTERPERSONAL RELATIONSHIPS:

Relationships suffer when individuals appear more interested in drinking than in sustaining their relationships: partners and children may feel that they have an implacable rival in alcohol.

Domestic discord and violence are common sequelae of alcohol misuse; alcohol is a major precipitating factor in as many as 40% of cases of domestic violence. Approximately one quarter of children reared in families where alcohol misuse is a major problem suffer from neglect and abuse. The children of problem drinkers are themselves more at risk than others of having psychological difficulties and drinking problems later in life. Indeed, doctors may only become aware of an individual's drinking problem as a result of its effects on the family. Violence is not the only manifestation of drunkenness that causes disruption to the family, and particularly to the children. When one parent is drinking excessively sole responsibility for all aspects of family life often falls to the other. When both parents are drinking this burden often falls to the older children. This leads to tension and psychological stress and eventually to family disintegration, although it is often surprising how long even the most dysfunctional of families stay together.

Parents who misuse alcohol often exhibit impulsive, erratic and unpredictable behaviour, which children cope with poorly. These children often have difficulties manifest as behavioural problems, poor performance at school and psychosomatic illnesses. It is clearly important that anyone who comes into contact with children from a household where alcohol is known to be a problem should look out for these problems. Equally it is important that appropriate enquiry is made about family dynamics, particularly the role of alcohol misuse, when assessing children with these behavioural difficulties.

When a doctor suspects that a child or an adult is the victim of domestic violence then it is clearly important to enquire about the potential role of alcohol. The fact that a partner or parent is misusing alcohol does not, of course, excuse the violence but it is important that the alcohol problem is tackled alongside the other issues involved. Child protection is of overriding importance.

PROBLEMS AT WORK:

Alcohol use and misuse cause a number of problems in the work place including absenteeism, inefficiency, impaired work performance and accidents. Current estimates indicate that in the UK alcohol is responsible for 3 to 5% of all absences from work, 17 million lost working days/annum and 20 to 25% of all industrial accidents. Nevertheless, alcohol plays a major role in the work-life of some sectors, for example, the media and the travel and hospitality industry, and is a major component of corporate entertainment.

Many organisations have *'Alcohol in Employment Policies'* aimed at minimizing the risks associated with inappropriate drinking amongst their work force *(Appendix D)*. These policies aim to ensure that drinking problems, once they come to light, are not viewed as a cause for disciplinary action or immediate dismissal. Rather affected employees are encouraged to seek appropriate help and their employment is secured during this process. This is clearly an important motivating factor in treatment. Employees who refuse to seek help and employees who do not make significant progress, once supported, will be subject to disciplinary proceedings. Occupational health nurses and physicians commonly play a major role in implementing a company's alcohol policy.

Most individuals with alcohol-related problems are employed. However, many individuals with significant alcohol-related problems will eventually lose their jobs. The effect of this will be determined, to a large extent, by family circumstances. Thus, if there is a second bread winner the family will often survive financially, at least to begin with, not just because they have another source of income but also because they have already adapted to the fact that much of the drinker's income will be spent on alcohol. Others are less fortunate. If there is no second income then considerable difficulties can arise if what money is available is spent on alcohol; this does not always happen as sometimes loss of employment can have a considerable 'sobering effect'. When, however, drinking continues in the face of significant financial hardship this almost invariably leads to a break down of relationships, which is often followed by loss of accommodation and a drift towards homelessness, unless appropriate help is obtained. Rehabilitation and recovery is much more difficult when conventional supports are lost.

CRIMINAL BEHAVIOUR:

Certain offences, such as underage drinking, drunkenness, drunk and disorderly and drink-driving are, by their very nature, alcohol-related.

The relative risk of a road traffic accident begins to increase with blood alcohol concentration as low as 20 mg/100 ml (4.3 mMol/l), is significant by 50 mg/100 ml (10.9 mMol/l) and highly significant by 100 mg/100 ml (21.7 mMol/l). It has been estimated that a quarter of individuals fatally injured in road traffic accidents have blood alcohol levels > 80 mg/100 ml (17.4 mMol/l). The dangers are particularly evident in young or inexperienced drivers. Most countries in Europe have adopted limits for driving of 50 mg/100 ml or less and there are proposals to lower the UK limit to this level.

Drinking also poses a hazard for most other forms of travel including rail, water and air and indeed being a pedestrian; it is reported that 37% of pedestrians killed on the roads have blood alcohol levels which exceed the legal limit for driving.

Alcohol may impair judgement, enrage passions and lead to anti-social behaviour, which is often concentrated in city centres and in areas of social deprivation. Drunkenness peaks in the teenage years. Truancy and school exclusion is related to alcohol misuse and a community's pre-occupation with drug-related crime may overlook a more widespread involvement of alcohol in disruptive behaviour. A quarter of young offenders entering prison report that they were intoxicated at the time of their offence.

Alcohol is a major factor in the commission of a variety of crimes including: criminal damage, theft, burglary, robbery and sexual and violent offences. Individuals who are chronically dependent on alcohol may steal the alcohol they cannot afford to buy or else may commit other crimes in order to obtain money to maintain their drinking habit, particularly to offset withdrawal symptoms. Almost 70% of men and 40% of women in prison have a history of hazardous drinking.

Accidents and injuries resulting from assaults, including facial injuries, are common and bear witness to the strong links between alcohol and violence. Nearly one-third of attendances at Accident and Emergency departments in the UK are alcohol-related, a figure that rises to near 70% during the night, particularly at weekends.

In the UK it is illegal to sell alcohol to anyone under the age of 18 years. There is a great deal of concern about underage drinking and the way in which younger people obtain and drink alcohol. Often they drink in public spaces such as parks, playgrounds and even on street corners; this frequently leads to noisy and disruptive behaviour and even violence. Various strategies have been adopted to combat this including creating drink-free zones within cities, where anyone drinking can be challenged and have their drink removed, or indeed be arrested, or, in the case of children, be reported to their parents. Off-sales staff and staff in licensed premises should be aware of the dangers of underage drinking and of the clearly delineated responsibilities they have in this regard.

SOCIAL DISINTEGRATION:

Some individuals with severe drinking problems lose their social and financial support and drift into vagrancy and homelessness. The 'skid row' problem drinker constitutes only a tiny minority of those with alcohol problems and considerable expertise and effort is required if they are to regain a more acceptable and less damaging way of life. Unfortunately, these individuals form the highly visible stereotype of the problem drinker and this can add further to their difficulties. It is known, for example, that medical staff are much more likely to identify alcohol problems in individuals who are 'down and out' than in individuals who are respectfully presented and socially adept.

The interactions between socioeconomic status and alcohol-related problems are complex. Although alcohol is a major casual factor there are other influences which heighten or diminish the risks of social disintegration. Thus, individuals who start their drinking career with good social and economic resources may remain protected from the consequences of excessive drinking for much longer than individuals who have little support and few resources. In consequence, these problems are commoner in areas of social deprivation.

PSYCHOLOGICAL PROBLEMS

Alcohol problems and major psychiatric illness may co-exist. Thus, psychiatric disorders occur in approximately 30% of individuals who are dependent on alcohol but in only 12% of the general population. In some patients the psychiatric illness apprears first while in others the psychological problems seem to develop as a direct consequence of prolonged excessive drinking. However, it is sometimes difficult to determine the exact sequence of events. There are, nevertheless, considerable differences in outcome between the two groups. Thus, patients with a primary psychiatric disorder who also misuse alcohol can be difficult to help as effective management requires the provision of integrated specialist services. Patients with schizophrenia, for example, require regular maintenance medication and follow-up which is much more difficult to facilitate if they are also misusing alcohol. In contrast, patients who develop psychiatric problems as a consequence of their alcohol misuse often improve considerably when alcohol is stopped without the need for major psychiatric intervention.

In some individuals abstinence may unmask features of depression, anxiety or difficulties in interpersonal relationships and, unless these problems are effectively dealt with, the prospects for long-term abstinence from alcohol are poor. These forms of psychological problem need attention in their own right and may well respond to appropriate psychological interventions or, in some circumstances, medication.

Drug and alcohol misuse often co-exist, particularly in the young, and this complicates assessment and treatment. Some individuals, in an attempt to self medicate, transfer their dependence from heroin to alcohol and *vice versa*. Dual dependence on alcohol and benzodiazepines is particularly common and the process of effecting withdrawal from both substances can be difficult and complex.

DEPRESSION:

There is a close link between alcohol misuse and depression. The biological changes induced in the brain by drinking alcohol mimic many of the changes evident in depressive mood disorders. It is also clear that the life of the problem drinker with anxieties about behaviour, and failing work performance, contributes to feelings of depression. In most circumstances the depression is secondary to the drinking problem so it would be wise for clinicians to persuade patients to stop drinking for a period of two or three weeks before reaching any conclusion about the presence and nature of any underlying psychological problems. During this time depression commonly lifts; 75% of a group of problem drinkers in one series had symptoms of depression at initial presentation, but only 5% reported persistent mood disturbance after 4 weeks of abstinence from alcohol.

In a minority of patients alcohol misuse is a symptom of an underlying depressive illness; these patients often have a family history of affective disorders. This link is more commonly found in women. Such individuals will need specialised input not only to deal with their alcohol misuse but also with their underlying mental health disorder.

Between 15 and 25% of all suicides in England and Wales are associated with alcohol misuse; almost 40% of men and 8% of women who attempt suicide are chronic problem drinkers. Completed suicide is much commoner in men. Self-harm is also common in younger, impulsive problem drinkers who tend to have a history of drug misuse.

Individuals with alcohol-related problems have a significant risk of suicide or self-harm particularly when these are associated with depression or social isolation (Table 4.1). All individuals misusing alcohol should, therefore, be questioned about suicidal behaviour and thoughts of self-harm and referred appropriately. Equally all individuals who attempt suicide should be carefully questioned about their drinking behaviour and appropriate referrals made.

ANXIETY:

Many individuals use alcohol as a means of coping with social and other anxieties and this may lead to harmful drinking. Patients with phobic anxiety states are particularly at risk of developing alcohol problems. In addition, the symptoms of alcohol withdrawal may mimic those of an anxiety state; thus, the dependent drinker may complain of feeling anxious and restless in the morning but the symptoms are relieved by drinking. It is, therefore, essential to enquire about drinking habits in patients presenting with symptoms suggestive of anxiety. The majority of anxiety symptoms associated with problem drinking disappear following abstinence from alcohol.

Table 4.1: The factors associated with an increased risk of suicide in heavy drinkers
Depressed mood
Severe intoxication
Associated drug misuse
Previous attempts
Impulsiveness
Recent interpersonal conflicts/losses
Unemployment
Loss of social supports

PERSONALITY DISORDERS:

Alcohol misuse may produce a pattern of behaviour which mimics that found in individuals with long-term personality disorders, although careful enquiry may reveal that the disorder was not present when the individual was abstinent or drinking in a less problematic way. Nonetheless, some individuals who misuse alcohol do have an underlying personality disorder although the numbers are thought to be small. These individuals often engage in anti-social and delinquent behaviour and do not seem to respond to conventional treatment approaches. Such individuals may spend several periods of time in prison without showing much evidence of change in their behaviour until advancing age or deteriorating health restrict their activities. It is very important, however, that the presence of a personality disorder is not regarded as a barrier to effecting change in drinking behaviour.

AMNESIA:

Episodes of amnesia for periods of hours or even days are a feature of alcohol misuse particularly following an episode of heavy drinking during which the blood alcohol level rises steeply. Alcoholic amnesias are experienced by a quarter of young men and 10% of young women during heavy drinking bouts, but if they occur at all frequently they are evidence of a serious alcohol problem. During these periods activities may be carried out in a purposeful way and the individual may not appear drunk. It appears as if memory traces of behaviour occurring at these times are not laid down, but the exact mechanism remains obscure.

ALCOHOLIC HALLUCINOSIS:

This is a relatively uncommon condition, which is characterized by the presence of hallucinations, usually auditory, occurring in clear consciousness. The hallucinations can occur either during a period of heavy drinking or following withdrawal or a sudden reduction in alcohol intake. They may take the form of non-specific noises or voices, whose utterances are often derogatory in nature, and appear to come from inside or from outside the head. Sometimes the hallucinations resemble those in schizophrenia in that they relate to the subject's actions and activities. The illness is usually self-limiting with resolution in one or two months. It is most important to reassure the patient about the nature of the condition, which can seem terrifying. In a small number of individuals there is progression to a state indistinguishable from schizophrenia. Symptoms are best treated with sulpiride or haloperidol, which can usually be stopped once the patient is symptom free.

PSYCHOTIC ILLNESSES:

Alcohol misuse may be associated with, or else may precipitate, psychotic illnesses such as schizophrenia. In these circumstances the prognosis is often not as good as for either condition alone, and management requires careful collaboration between specialist services.

MORBID JEALOUSY:

Morbid jealousy refers to a state in which an individual, almost invariably a man, develops a delusional belief that his partner is being unfaithful. The victim is beset by accusations of infidelity; a search is frequently made for incriminating evidence and they may be followed or attempts made to catch them 'in the act'. Victims may be in real physical danger and on occasions there have been tragic, sometimes fatal, results. This syndrome is found in problem drinkers, but it may occur in a range of psychiatric conditions, or indeed as a syndrome in its own right.

COGNITIVE IMPAIRMENT

Alcohol is neurotoxic and when taken to excess causes cognitive impairment. Paradoxically, there is some evidence that moderate consumption in later life is associated with reduced risk of cognitive decline. There is also evidence that in some situations alcohol may be neuroprotective. Thus, individuals who suffer head trauma having consumed low to moderate amounts of alcohol may suffer less in the way of neurological consequences than their sober counterparts.

Individuals with a history of alcohol misuse may show evidence of cerebral atrophy with enlargement of the cerebral ventricles and widening of the cerebral sulci on cerebral imaging (Plate 4.1). At post-mortem the brains of these individuals are smaller and lighter in weight. Although there is some evidence of actual neuronal loss and dendritic shrinkage, particularly in the frontal cortex, cerebellum and hypothalamus, the major abnormality is a reduction in white matter volume as a result of loss of myelin and axonal integrity. The white matter changes and the dendritic shrinkage resolve, to a significant extent, following absence from alcohol. In consequence significant improvement may be observed in the appearances on cerebral imaging.

These morphological findings are often accompanied by features of cognitive decline, particularly abstract problem solving, visuospatial and visual learning, memory function and perceptual motor skills; these features are considered to be 'frontal' in nature. Abstinence from alcohol is associated with improvement particularly in working memory, problem solving and attention span.

The term alcohol-related dementia is used to describe these changes in cognition in individuals with a history of alcohol misuse but the term dementia implies a chronic progressive disorder which this is not; abstinence is associated with improvement in cerebral function and even continued drinking may not be associated with progressive decline. As a result there is considerable debate about the terminology of this condition.

The impairment observed in cognitive function may vary from mild to severe and does not necessarily 'match' the degree of cerebral atrophy observed on imaging. The differential diagnoses include the progressive dementias and Korsakov's psychosis, although the memory deficits in the latter are more specific. In addition, other conditions which are commonly observed in patients with a history of alcohol misuse, such as recurrent head trauma and the consequences of poorly controlled fitting need to be considered, together with hepatic encephalopathy in individuals with alcohol-related cirrhosis.

The diagnosis rests on observing significant cognitive impairment without profound amnestic change in an individual with a history of chronic excessive drinking of at least 5 years duration, including significant consumption in the past 3 years. It is also important to reassess the patient after a period of abstinence of at least 60 days to look for signs of improvement before confirming the diagnosis.

Treatment is based on the maintenance of abstinence from alcohol, on the provision of adequate social support and on recapturing social and self-care skills. Memory rehabilitation techniques and external memory aids such as 'reminder message' paging are helpful; redesigning the environment to include memory cues and aids to orientation are also beneficial. Improvement is often detectable over prolonged periods and regular review is essential.

Plate 4.1: Cerebral Atrophy

Cerebral CT scan in a healthy 61 year old man.

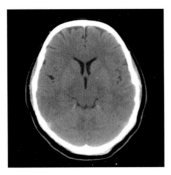

Cerebral CT scan in a 61 year old man with a long history of alcohol misuse. There is evidence of significant cerebral atrophy with prominent sulci and dilated ventricules ⤢ .

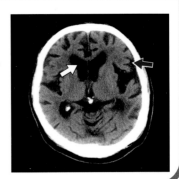

LEARNING POINTS

Social Problems:

- Social problems are a common and often early sign of harmful drinking.

- Acute intoxication is associated with public disorder, accidents and criminal behaviour.

- Chronic alcohol misuse causes family, legal, occupational and psychological problems.

- Children from 'drinking households' have a higher than average risk of future problem drinking.

- Alcohol is a major cause of absenteeism from work, lost productivity and industrial accidents.

- Alcohol is a major factor in the commission of a variety of crimes; over half the prison population have a history of hazardous drinking.

Psychological Problems:

- Psychiatric co-morbidity is very common in problem drinkers.

- Many psychological problems resolve spontaneously when drinking ceases, particularly depression and anxiety.

- Individuals misusing alcohol should always be assessed for the risk of self-harm.

- Individuals who have self-harmed should always be asked about their drinking behaviour.

- Cognitive impairment arising in the context of alcohol misuse is difficult to assess until after a period of abstinence from alcohol.

CHAPTER 5

THE DETECTION AND ASSESSMENT OF ALCOHOL MISUSE

Many patients will present with a drinking problem that is all too obvious. Others, however, will present less obviously or else with no suggestion of excessive drinking at first encounter. It is clearly important to identify individuals drinking at hazardous or harmful levels as early as possible in the hope of intervening before the drinking behaviour produces problems. It is equally important to fully assess individuals presenting with alcohol-related physical or psychological problems in order to best meet their treatment needs.

A variety of methods are employed to unearth the unwary drinker and to apprise individuals who are all too aware that they have a drinking problem. Some methods, for example, taking an alcohol history, are used routinely in all clinical settings. Others, for example, the screening questionnaires, are used more frequently for population screening than in day-to-day clinical practice.

DRINKING HISTORY

The majority of individuals in Great Britain drink sensibly, most of the time. However, approximately 38% of men and 16% of women have an alcohol use disorder while some 6% of men and 2% of women are alcohol dependent. Many individuals are unaware of how much they drink and its potential impact on their health. It is, therefore, important to obtain an alcohol history from all patients when first encountered and periodically thereafter. However, although individuals who present with a drinking problem are often quizzed about their drinking antecedents, the histories taken from others are perfunctory and do not provide sufficient information to adequately judge past and present drinking behaviour.

Questions should be phrased in a matter-of-fact but tactful and professional way. Thus, individuals should be asked how many times a week they take an alcoholic drink and how much they drink on each occasion. This process is facilitated by use of a drinking diary (Figure 5.1). Provided that the record is representative of 'usual' consumption then a weekly total in units can be calculated (*Appendix A*). Patients who drink solely at home are able to give better estimates of their alcohol intake, as they will be directly responsible for its purchase. Individuals who drink in company and/or in public places may have greater difficulty in providing an accurate record as they may buy only a proportion of the alcohol they consume or else may only consume a proportion of the alcohol they buy.

Individuals drinking in the 'low-risk' range, that is, ≤21 units/week for men and ≤14 units/week for women, spread evenly over the week, with 2 to 3 drink-free days, should then be asked whether there were times when they drank more regularly or heavily than at present. Provided that the answer does not raise any particular concerns then nothing more will be required. They may benefit from information about the unit system and should be advised to check on their own intake periodically using a drinking diary. Individuals identified as drinking in a hazardous or harmful way need to be questioned further. Before doing so it is important to realise that although it is often alleged that such individuals deliberately and consistently under-report their alcohol intake it is also likely that they genuinely can not remember exactly how much they were drinking 5, 10 or 20 years ago.

It is useful to obtain a brief inventory of the individual's major life events, at the outset, to use for referencing or prompting when taking the actual drinking history. Thus, information should be sought on the age at which they left school, further education or vocational training, employment and dates of major events such as marriage, births of children, divorce and deaths of close relatives. It is useful at this time to enquire about the drinking habits of partners and family members.

Figure 5.1: Sample drinking diary

Week commencing ....

Day (date)	Beverage	Amount	Circumstances (where, when, with whom)	Units
			Weekly Total:	

Using this information as a background an attempt should be made to determine the age of onset of a regular pattern of daily or weekly drinking, independently of the amount consumed; the age of onset of alcohol misuse, defined as the establishment of a pattern of regular drinking in excess of 60 g (7.5 units) daily for men and 40 g (5 units) daily for women; and details of the current drinking behaviour. If the individual reports a pattern of 'binge' drinking then details should be obtained about the length of each 'binge', the amount of alcohol consumed during the 'binge', the time periods between 'binges', the drinking behaviour between 'binges' and possible precipitating factors for drinking.

Evidence of physical dependence on alcohol should always be sought because of its management implications; early morning retching, tremor, anxiety and irritability, ingestion of alcohol before midday, amnesia and 'blackouts' are all suggestive; the occurrence, severity and treatment of any previous episodes of alcohol withdrawal should be recorded. Information should always be obtained on previous advice, counselling or other treatments received for the alcohol problem.

Although an alcohol history should be obtained as soon after first contact with the individual as possible, it may be necessary to postpone taking a detailed history if they have features of alcohol withdrawal or are receiving medication to prevent their occurrence. Ideally, the history should be taken on more than one occasion, preferably by more than one person; this is particularly usefully done when the results of the various investigations are to hand. Confirmation of the alcohol history should always be obtained, provided the patient is agreeable, from as many alternative sources as possible.

ADDITIONAL HISTORY

Initial enquiry should be made into the individual's *domestic, social, financial* and *employment* situations. It is important to try to gauge the degree of support they might receive from family and friends in their endeavours to achieve and maintain control of their drinking behaviour. It is important to find out whether their job is safe or in jeopardy, or, if they are unemployed, what their employment prospects are likely to be. The financial burden of their alcohol habit is likely to have been substantial and many will have serious financial problems. Careful enquiry should also be made into any dealings they may have had with the law, for even the most 'respectable' may have 'proceedings pending' (*Appendix B*). All of these factors must be taken into account when devising a management plan.

Careful and sensitive enquiry should be made about the patient's current *psychological* status; it is particularly important to elucidate feelings of anxiety, panic, depression and suicidal ideation. Details of any previous psychiatric illnesses should be sought and all previous investigations and treatments of relevance should be carefully documented.

Many patients, even those with established alcohol-related *physical* disease, may be asymptomatic or only complain of non-specific symptoms, usually referable to the gastrointestinal tract. A history of specific symptoms should be sought. Details of all previous investigations and treatment should be obtained.

PHYSICAL EXAMINATION

Individuals may present with evidence of recent alcohol consumption; they may smell of alcohol; they may be flushed with blood-shot eyes, excitable and tremulous or even overtly intoxicated. Alternatively they may appear sober, rational and in every way unexceptional.

On examination they may show a constellation of cutaneous and other superficial abnormalities indicative of chronic alcohol misuse including spider naevi, cutaneous telan-giectasia, palmar erythema, Dupuytren's contractures, facial mooning, parotid enlargement and gynaecomastia (Chapter 3). There may also be evidence of alcohol-related harm such as injuries either new or old, systemic hypertension, hepatomegaly or peripheral neuropathy. Alternatively they may show few, if any, relevant clinical signs.

LABORATORY INVESTIGATIONS

A number of abnormalities in laboratory test results may be observed. The three most commonly identified, and indeed most frequently used markers of alcohol misuse, are elevation of the erythrocyte mean corpuscular volume (MCV) and increases in serum aspartate aminotransferase (AST) and gamma glutamyl transpeptidase (GGT) activities. None of these markers is sufficiently sensitive or specific enough to be used in isolation but the combination provides useful collaborative evidence of alcohol misuse both initially and for subsequent monitoring. Serum AST and GGT activities return to within the reference range after approximately 2 to 4 weeks of abstinence from alcohol but the erythrocyte MCV may remain elevated for upwards of 3 months. Persistent elevation of the serum AST and GGT, despite abstinence from alcohol, is likely to reflect the presence of underlying liver disease. Hyperuricaemia and hypertriglyceridaemia are also commonly observed, particularly in men.

The role of serum carbohydrate deficient transferrin (CDT) as a marker of alcohol misuse and for monitoring abstinence remains unclear. Serum CDT values often rise in individuals who have consumed at least 60 g of alcohol daily for a minimum of 2 week and normalize after 4 to 6 weeks of abstinence. However, false positive results have been reported in patients with non-alcoholic liver disease, coeliac disease, iron-deficiency anaemia, congenital disorders of glycosylation and in individuals taking oestrogens and possibly anti-epileptic medication. Equally, false negative results have been reported in varying proportions of heavy drinkers and individuals abusing alcohol. In addition, the test results obtained are highly dependent on the method used for quantification. Many different analytical techniques are in use and the inter-method variability can be considerable. The best methods are both expensive and generally difficult to access. Serum CDT is not used in routine clinical practice in the UK; in some countries it is used in the appraisal of licence applications following a drink-drive conviction and for work place screening.

A number of ethanol-specific metabolites, for example ethyl glucuronide, can be detected in urine and hair but their measurement is difficult and at present confined to forensic practice.

The presence of alcohol-related organ damage may be reflected by a number of other laboratory abnormalities; thus individuals with significant liver disease are likely to have hyperbilirubinaemia, hypoalbuminaemia and a prolonged prothrombin time, while individuals with pancreatitis may have hyperamylasaemia. Further investigations should be undertaken, as indicated, to assess the full extent of any associated alcohol-related physical harm.

SCREENING QUESTIONNAIRES

A number of screening questionnaires have been developed to facilitate detection of excessive drinking. They vary in complexity, the ways in which they are administered, the level of alcohol misuse they are designed to detect and the populations in which they have been validated, and hence in whom their use is applicable (Table 5.1; *Appendix C*).

The best known of these screening questionnaires is the **CAGE**, which is an acronym for the four questions posed:

1   Have you ever felt that you ought to **C**ut down on your drinking?

2   Have people ever **A**nnoyed you by asking about your drinking?

3   Have you ever felt bad or **G**uilty about your drinking?

4   Have you ever had a drink first thing in the morning (**E**ye-opener) to steady your nerves or get rid of a hangover?

The CAGE is simple to remember and easy and quick to administer. It is not useful for detecting hazardous drinking *per se* but a score of two or more is suggestive of dependent drinking. This is probably the most commonly administered questionnaire in routine clinical practice.

The Michigan Alcoholism Screening Test **(MAST)** is one of the oldest alcohol screening instruments and has been used extensively in a variety of populations and settings with a reported sensitivity for detecting 'alcoholism' of greater than 90%. However, because it focuses on problems over the patient's lifetime, rather than on recent events, it is less likely to detect alcohol problems at an early stage. In addition, the original test, which included 25 items, later reduced to 22 items, was time consuming to undertake, making it unsuitable for use in busy medical

Table 5.1: Alcohol screening questionnaires		
Screening Tool *Reference*	Acronym expanded	Description
CAGE *Mayfield et al, 1974*	Acronym devised from key words in questions	Four items: self administered/interview
MAST *Selzer, 1968*	Michigan Alcohol Screening Test	22 items ; self- administered/interview
SMAST *Selzer, 1975*	Short version of MAST	13 items; self- administered/interview
MAST-G *Blow, 1991*	Geriatric version of MAST	24 items; designed for older adults; self- administered/interview
SMAST-G *Blow et al, 1998*	Geriatric version of SMAST	10 items; designed for older adults; self- administered/interview
AUDIT *Babor et al, 1989*	Alcohol Use Disorders Identification Test	10 items; self- administered/interview
FAST *Hodgson et al, 2002*	Fast Alcohol Screening Test	Questions 3 ,5, 8 and 10 of the AUDIT; self- administered/interview
PAT *Smith et al, 1996*	Paddington Alcohol Test	Three items; self- administered/interview: A&E departments
T-ACE *Sokol et al, 1989*	Acronym devised from key words in questions	Four items: self administered/interview: Prenatal/antenatal

A number of very brief screening questionnaire have been developed to identify hazardous drinking, as well as alcohol-related harm and dependence, in busy medical settings such as the Accident and Emergency department, fracture clinics and primary care. The Paddington Alcohol Test **(PAT)** was developed specifically for use in Accident and Emergency departments while the Fast Alcohol Screening Test **(FAST)**, which is a shortened version of the AUDIT, was designed for use in all settings where time pressure is a major factor. Both questionnaires can be administered in under a minute and show good sensitivity and specificity when compared with other more lengthy screening instruments. The **T-ACE** questionnaire, which is a modified version of the CAGE, is useful for prenatal/antenatal screening.

It is clearly important to detect hazardous and harmful drinking as early as possible. The simplest way is to take an alcohol history from all patients when first encountered. However, this is often done badly, if at all. Laboratory markers and screening questionnaires can facilitate detection of a substantial proportion of individuals misusing alcohol both in primary care and in the hospital setting.

LEARNING POINTS

- Individuals drinking at hazardous or harmful levels should be identified as early as possible.

- It is mandatory to take an alcohol history from every patient encountered in the clinical setting.

- Screening questionnaires can be used to facilitate detection of alcohol misuse. They vary in the level of misuse they are designed to detect and the populations in which they have been validated.

- A combination of measurements of the serum AST, serum GGT and erythrocyte MCV provide a sensitive index for the detection and monitoring of drinking behaviour.

- All individuals misusing alcohol should be assessed for evidence of alcohol-related psychological and physical harm.

setting. Thus, several shorter versions of the MAST have been developed over time, including the 13-item short MAST **(SMAST)**. Geriatric versions, the **MAST-G** and **SMAST-G**, were designed specifically for use in older adults. All versions of the MAST can be self-administered or completed at interview.

The Alcohol Use Disorders Identification Test **(AUDIT)** was developed, under the auspices of the World Health Organisation, for use in primary care. It was designed to provide information on drinking behaviour in the preceding year with the aim of identifying hazardous drinkers at risk of developing alcohol-related problems. The questionnaire is simple, quick and easy to complete and can be self-administered or administered by non-clinical staff. It is said to allow detection of hazardous drinking earlier, and with greater sensitivity, than either the CAGE or MAST questionnaires, or routine admission clerking.

CHAPTER 6

THE MANAGEMENT OF ALCOHOL MISUSE

Individuals drinking in a hazardous or harmful way should be offered help with their drinking problem. This can be provided in a variety of settings by a variety of people.

Many individuals, particularly those drinking in a hazardous way, may require little more than simple advice provided in the form of a brief intervention perhaps in a primary care setting. Individuals drinking in a harmful way will usually require additional help. Some will access self-help groups such as Alcoholic Anonymous (AA) or local Alcohol Advice Services, which offer a wide range of services, including counselling. Some drinkers will seek help from their primary care physician and may then be referred to a Community Alcohol Team. Others, primarily those with severe dependence and co-existent physical or psychiatric morbidity, will require referral for specialist consultant care. Most of these individuals can be treated as out-patients. In-patient treatment may be necessary for a minority to allow controlled withdrawal from alcohol and further assessment. In some circumstances, for example, when there is little or no social support or there are problems with accommodation, more prolonged residential care will be necessary.

Most individuals with drinking problems hope that they will be able to regain controlled social drinking. However, **abstinence** from alcohol is the preferred aim in older individuals, those who have exhibited serious physical dependency on alcohol, those with significant alcohol-related physical harm and those who have previously failed to modify their drinking behaviour, despite advice. If the family is very strongly against any attempt at controlled drinking, or if the environment is such that relapse seems extremely likely, then the aim should also be for abstinence. For some patients, particularly those who are younger and those who have little evidence of physical harm, **controlled** or **modified drinking** *may* be an appropriate option.

The level and type of support an individual requires may not be obvious on first encounter and it does not follow that the individuals who seemingly have the most severe problems will necessarily need the most support. Thus, it is difficult to be too prescriptive about how these individuals should be managed although general guidelines can be provided (Figure 6.1). It is also important to remember that some individuals may not wish to engage with services and allowance must be made for this; the key is flexibility. For this reason, it is still useful to detail the types of therapy available and the settings in which they may be provided separately although the divide is somewhat artificial.

AVAILABLE TREATMENTS

PSYCHOLOGICAL THERAPY

Brief Intervention

The term 'brief intervention' is used to describe a range of time-limited interventions, which commonly last from 5 to 20 minutes. These techniques are usually focused on individuals drinking at hazardous levels. They can, however, be used in individuals drinking at harmful levels, once they have been successfully withdrawn from alcohol, if they are motivated to maintain abstinence and are well supported in these endeavours. There are no hard and fast rules.

A brief intervention usually consists of an assessment of recent alcohol intake, the provision of information on hazardous/ harmful drinking, clear specific advice on options supported by relevant literature and contact details of local agencies. Such an approach must be delivered in an empathic, non-judgemental, and understandable way. Raising awareness at a critical time, for example following admission to hospital, may be helpful in facilitating behavioural change.

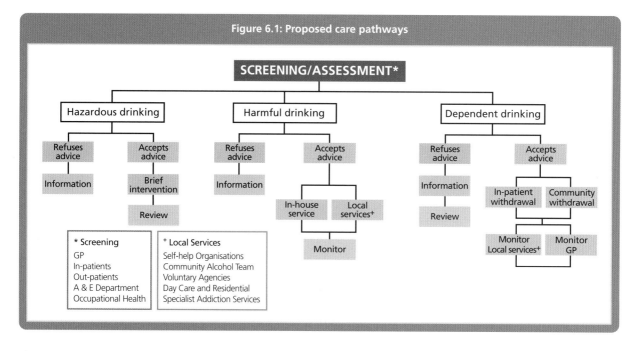

Figure 6.1: Proposed care pathways

This approach is now being used in a range of different clinical settings and there is good evidence that it reduces hazardous/harmful drinking behaviours. Once motivation has been effected, further change may be relatively easy to achieve. Follow-up may help to consolidate the changes achieved.

It is first important to understand the individual's current view of their own drinking and their attitude towards making change. This crucial stage is often best addressed by an approach known as *motivational interviewing*. This is a technique that assists the individual to arrive at their own decision about changing their habits. The clinician should always be positive about the changes envisaged, stressing the benefits and offering suggestions for strategies for change. Some individuals seen in hospital and primary health care settings will respond well to simple advice, and it is always worth using this as a first approach. Others will require more help in making a commitment to change.

It is important to remember that while it might be clear to everyone else concerned that an individual needs to change their drinking behaviour, they may not share this point of view. Often, individuals will acquiesce to a doctor's opinion while not truly incorporating the advice they are given. The individual's own views of their drinking habits and problems must be elicited. They may

not have thought seriously about changing their drinking behaviour. In these circumstances the first task is to provide information and feedback about the risks associated with their current alcohol intake and about any associated health problems that may have already arisen. At this stage it is helpful to make it clear that the onus lies with the individual to make the necessary change, and only when they are willing to accept this first step is it appropriate to give advice about strategies for cutting down and achieving a less harmful level of drinking. There is no merit in argument or confrontation; it is best to roll with any resistances and help the individual develop their own balance sheet of the pros and cons of changing their drinking habits (Table 6.1). The essential components of motivational interviewing and brief interventions of this kind have been summarized with the acronym FRAMES (Table 6.2).

Barriers to change

Habits are difficult to change. Most of us will be able to recognise this from our own experience of trying to change a well-established habit, whether eating too much or too little, changing diet, smoking, exercise or other lifestyle issues. Many problem drinkers will find that much of their life is dominated by the need to drink and many barriers to change will have to be confronted (Table 6.3); the following are the most important:

Dependence: This may be physical or psychological; those who are physically dependent will have to be carefully withdrawn from alcohol (Chapter 7); those who are psychologically dependent will need to identify triggers to drinking and find new ways of dealing with craving and alternative ways of coping. They could, for example, devise techniques for refusing drinks and rehearse them with family and friends until they feel comfortable; they could also develop and adopt diversionary activities, in thought or action, for times of particular difficulty. Some individuals may need more formal help to cope with their psychological dependence; social skills and cognitive behavioural therapy, arranged by specialist alcohol services, are often very helpful.

Stress: For some individuals this is a major barrier to making change; they regularly use alcohol to deal with difficult situations in their lives. Counselling and other forms of psychological help such as cognitive behavioural therapy may be necessary to overcome this problem. Self-help manuals are often useful for learning relaxation and stress management techniques.

The patient's **environment** can be a barrier to change; for example, they may have a job where selling or entertaining brings them into regular contact with alcohol, or their social life may be constructed around drinking occasions.

Habit: Never underestimate the force of habits as they can be extremely difficult to break. The individual needs to identify occasions when they have been 'in the habit' of having a drink, for example, at particular times of day, in particular company or situations. Keeping a diary is often a good means of identifying these risky times (Figure 5.1). They can then agree a plan, with their practioner, for dealing with these situations, and then review how successfully they have been overcome.

Occasionally alcohol will have been used as a form of self-mediation to cope with **psychiatric** or **physical illness**. In these circumstances, the underlying condition must be identified and treated along with the alcohol problem so that the individual gains confidence in coping with their illness without recourse to drinking.

The **influence of others** is, for many, a powerful factor. This influence may either be *positive*, for example, support and encouragement during times of potential

TABLE 6.1: Sample balance sheet of drinking options

	Likely Consequences of Drinking		
	Continuing	Reducing	Stopping
PROS of chosen course. Use the phrase 'what appears good?'	Forget my worries (for a time) Keep my drinking friends	Be like others Not be a kill-joy at social events	Family want me to Doctor says it is the only way my liver will recover Save a lot of money
CONS of chosen course. Use the phrase 'what appears not so good?'	Partner may leave Children very upset Lose my job Liver failure	Didn't work when I tried before Partner wouldn't believe me Liver still being damaged	Could I cope with social events and celebrations? Feel un-comfortable with my friends

TABLE 6.2: The essential components of motivational interviewing and a brief intervention

FRAMES

- **F**eedback about the risk of personal harm or impairment
- Stress personal **R**esponsibility for making change
- **A**dvice to cut down or, if necessary, stop drinking
- Provide a **M**enu of alternative strategies for changing drinking patterns
- **E**mpathic interviewing style
- **S**elf efficacy: an intuitive style which leaves the patient enhanced in feeling able to cope with the goals they have agreed

Source: *Bien et al, Addiction1993; **88**: 315-335*

relapse, or else *negative,* for example encouraging and cajoling them to drink. It is often helpful to rehearse dealing with such pressure, either at individual interviews or as part of a social skills management group.

A final barrier to change is a sense of **hopelessness** or **pessimism**. The drinker may feel that it is impossible for them to change their drinking behaviour. Equally, the practitioner may feel pessimistic about the likelihood that a given individual will succeed in attaining this goal or else have broader concerns, for example, about their own ability to provide the individual with the support they need to successfully effect change. These feelings are often based on a few unrewarding experiences; it is easy to forget that the majority of problem drinkers respond well to help and advice.

At the end of the interview the individual should be clear about why their drinking is of concern. They should have a clear idea of the risks of continuing to drink at their present level and of the benefits of changing their behaviour. They should have been helped to formulate clear goals, to have identified the means for change and decided the time frame within which to achieve it. They should also have been made aware of the likely barriers to change and of potential ways of overcoming them.

At the end of the interview it is important to have:

Set goals: Goals should be *specific, attainable, short-term,* and preferably *immediately rewarding.* They should be defined and agreed by the individual; a written record should be provided to help reinforce resolve.

Involve the family: Family distress is common and encouraging family members to join in the interview is a useful way of reinforcing the decisions made. Identify those who are supportive and the form that this support takes. Specific friends may also help in this respect. Remember that confidentiality must be respected and any approach to others must be with the individual's agreement.

Identify any underlying physical or psychiatric problems: It is important to ensure that underlying significant physical and/or psychiatric problems are identified so that the necessary investigations and treatment can be instigated.

Identify significant barriers to change: It is also important to identify those aspects of the individual's attitudes, problems and concerns that may pose a significant barrier to change. In some instances social skills training or cognitive behavioural therapy might help overcome some of the difficulties.

Above all, **engender a positive approach:** Aim to enhance the individual's self esteem and sense of being able to cope. Emphasise your confidence in their ability to effect change.

Often the individual will respond well to the advice given and only brief but regular follow-up will be necessary; monitoring

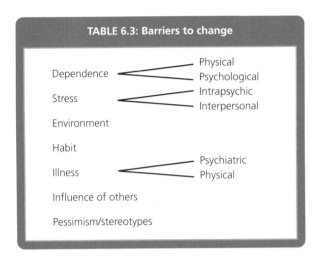

TABLE 6.3: Barriers to change

Dependence	Physical / Psychological
Stress	Intrapsychic / Interpersonal
Environment	
Habit	
Illness	Psychiatric / Physical
Influence of others	
Pessimism/stereotypes	

progress with regular blood tests to estimate the serum AST, serum GGT and erythrocyte MCV is also helpful as the results can be used to provide feedback for reinforcement. If the interview has taken place in a hospital setting, then the general practitioner should be told what advice has been given so that it can be followed up at a later stage.

In some circumstances the individual will be unable to make the anticipated changes and may need further help. This may be because some of the barriers to change have proven insurmountable in the first instance and will require more detailed attention. Drinkers who are physically dependent may need help to withdraw from alcohol before any changes are possible. Drinkers with significant alcohol-related physical disease may need hospital admission to address these problems at an early stage.

COGNITIVE AND BEHAVIOURAL THERAPIES

These encompass a range of approaches in which the individual works collaboratively with a therapist towards achieving specific treatment goals. These techniques can be used to facilitate changes in drinking behaviour and also in relapse prevention.

Cognitive behavioural therapy is typically provided by a psychologist or appropriately trained nurse. The individual learns to identify triggers to drinking and to find new ways of coping with them. It may be combined with social skills training to develop competence in handling previously high-risk situations.

Solution focused relapse prevention therapy in which the therapist and drinker together identify and practice strategies for avoiding relapse. The emphasis is on the solution rather than the problem.

Stress management and relaxation training aimed at reducing overall levels of stress and anxiety.

Counselling which generally seeks to clarify psychosocial factors underlying alcohol misuse and finding other less destructive ways of dealing with them.

Family/couples therapy enlists family, most often the partner, in supporting and at the same time monitoring and challenging the drinker. The process aims to help develop more supportive and less dysfunctional relationships.

PHARMACOTHERAPY

Drug therapy may be directed at controlling alcohol misuse *per se*. Currently three drugs are licensed for this indication. The best known of these is the so-called alcohol-sensitising agent, *disulfiram* (Antabuse). This drug is an inhibitor of hepatic ALDH; if individuals taking this drug imbibe alcohol their blood acetaldehyde concentrations increase significantly, producing a flushing reaction, which may be accompanied by nausea, vomiting, tachycardia, hypotension, dyspnoea, dizziness, and headache. This reaction varies in intensity depending on the amount of alcohol taken; the combination of this agent with alcohol can be severe and even fatal.

The overall efficacy of disulfiram is difficult to judge. Its use is absolutely contraindicated during pregnancy and in patients with florid psychoses and established hyper-sensitivity. It should not be used in patients with seriously impaired cardiac, respiratory, hepatic or cerebral function; it is relatively contraindicated in patients with diabetes, epilepsy and hypercholesterolaemia. In all circumstances its use should be carefully explained to the patient who should be provided with a card detailing the nature of the therapeutic regimen. Individuals should be in control of their own treatment but there are benefits in agreeing a contract whereby a relative, close friend or work colleague witnesses the taking of the medication. *This drug should never be given to a patient without their knowledge or consent.*

In recent years a number of new pharmacotherapeutic approaches to the treatment of alcohol misuse have been developed based on knowledge of the effects of chronic alcohol misuse on cerebral neurotransmitter systems and neurotransmitter balance. To date, most pharmacological approaches to the treatment of alcohol dependence have focused on modifying the activity of the specific neurotransmitters thought to be involved in the regulation of alcohol consumption.

The opiate receptor antagonist *naltrexone* has been shown to have a significant but modest effect on drinking behaviour in carefully selected patients admitted to intensive treatment programmes. It is usually prescribed in a daily dose of 50 mg and is given for 3 to 4 months. A depot IM preparation is also available, which is given monthly for up to 6 months. Patients do better if they are abstinent at the start of treatment. Outcome might relate, at least in part, to the presence of a functional variant allele in the μ opioid receptor. Approximately 30% of patients taking naltrexone experience mild gastrointestinal and constitutional side-effects early in treatment. However, significant hepatotoxicity has been reported with higher dosage regimens particularly in obese individuals. It takes 48 to 72 hours for the anti-opiate effects to wear off after oral dosing and up to 6 weeks following depot injection. Problems may, therefore, arise if patients taking naltrexone are inadvertently given opiates or need opiates, for example following surgery or accidental injury. The drug is clearly contraindicated in current opiate users. Naltrexone is used widely in the North America and Europe but is not licensed currently for use in the UK.

The functional glutamate antagonist *acamprosate* (calcium acetylhomotaurinate) also has a significant, albeit modest, effect on drinking behaviour but the benefits of treatment increase over time. It is usually prescribed in a daily divided dose of 2 g and given for 12 to 18 months. Greatest benefit is seen if treatment is started just before the patient is withdrawn from alcohol. Acamprosate has an excellent safety profile; a small number of patients experience mild and usually transient gastrointestinal or dermatological side-effects but no major side-effects have been reported, in particular there is no reported hepatotoxicity. Acamprosate is licensed for use in Europe, Australasia and North America.

A number of other agents, including *baclofen, ondansetron* and *topiramate* have been proposed for the treatment of alcohol dependence but none is yet used in general clinical practice in the UK.

As the pathogenesis of alcohol dependence is further unravelled other targets for treatment will be identified. The differential efficacy of these various agents may well be explained by differences in pharmacogenetics. Thus, in time, it is likely that the choice of therapy will be governed by the patient's pharmacogenetic profile.

Treatment may be required for an underlying psychiatric illness. Great care must be taken to evaluate the patient fully before making a judgement about the coexistence of an affective disorder. If depression is evident then treatment with conventional antidepressants may be helpful although patients should be monitored very carefully. Occasionally, alcohol misuse may accompany hypomania, which may be effectively treated, even in this setting, with major tranquillisers and occasionally lithium, if not otherwise contraindicated.

SELF-HELP GROUPS/FACILITIES

Alcoholics Anonymous (AA) is the best-known self-help group in the world. The AA programme offers hope, fellowship and clear simple advice about changing habits. They provide a twelve-step recovery programme with abstinence as a goal. AA members help others by sharing their experience of their own drinking problem and their road to recovery. They will usually meet newcomers personally and introduce them to a local meeting.

AlAnon is a parallel organisation for the partners, relatives and friends of problem drinkers and offers an opportunity for mutual support and understanding. Membership does not require the partner to attend AA or even to admit to having an alcohol problem.

AlAteen, is a somewhat similar organisation for the teenage children of problem drinkers, although not as widely available; it offers children a chance to share some of the anxieties and problems they often experience.

A number of on-line websites are now available which provide information on drinking levels and advice about harm reduction. Most use information on current drinking behaviour to calculate weekly intakes and to categorize drinking behaviour. Some sites give simple advice based on the information provided; others provide more structured advice and can be used to monitor changes in drinking behaviour. These websites are becoming increasingly popular: examples include:

http://units.nhs.uk/unitCalculator.html;
http://units.nhs.uk/cuttingDown.html
http://www.bupa.co.uk/health_information/asp/
healthy_living/lifestyle/alcohol/alctest.asp

TREATMENT DELIVERY

Treatment can be delivered either within the community or else by specialist addiction services. However, as the range of therapies provided in both settings is similar the boundaries between these services are noticeably blurred. Many 'specialist' services are in fact situated within Primary Care settings, with teams of non-medical staff, employed by a mixture of service providers, including the NHS, social services and the voluntary sector. In addition, general practitioners are now playing a more active and hence more important role in the management of patients with addictive behaviours.

COMMUNITY-BASED SERVICES

The availability and nature of local community services and the way in which they are accessed and funded varies considerably across the country. Thus, it is important to know what local services are available and their accessibility within the referral pathway. Each service should have clearly specified aims and should provide information on its programme content, quality standards and outcomes.

The network of services needs to be managed and monitored by a strategic planning team partnership which should include all the relevant stakeholders: health; social work; the voluntary sector; and user groups, including family and carer representatives. It is important to ensure that there is ready movement of clients/patients between the different provisions and that bureaucratic and professional boundaries are not allowed to impede the path to recovery.

Onward referral can be viewed as rejection by someone to whom a confidence and trust has been given. Thus, whenever a referral is made to another agency a follow-up appointment for the referring service should also be given. Transitions between agencies need to be handled with care because many individuals are lost to follow-up at this stage.

The range and character of the services available should be based on a preliminary community needs assessment but typically might include:

Community Alcohol Team: These have been established in many areas and provide assessment, brief intervention, follow-up and support. Specialist Community Psychiatric Nurses (CPN) with skills in assessment, alcohol withdrawal and relapse prevention techniques play an important role, working as part of a community team but linking with Primary Health Care services.

Counselling and Advice Services: These are also provided by Councils on Alcohol and other voluntary agencies.

Social Services: These play an important part in assessing alcohol problems and arranging necessary help, support and rehabilitation. Alcohol misuse causes major disruption to family life and it is essential that the needs of partners and children are taken into account within the range of community services.

Day Centre and Residential Services: These provide longer-term support for individuals who need time and additional help in retaining sobriety while re-establishing themselves in society, for example, those who are debilitated and those who have lost their support networks. Residential care is often necessary for homeless problem drinkers including those who are making the difficult transition from prison back into the community. Patients suffering from alcohol-related brain damage may require long-term residential support and specialist services to ensure that they achieve optimum recovery.

SPECIALIST ADDICTION SERVICES

There are a number of NHS addiction services, which are usually staffed by a consultant psychiatrist, clinical psychologists, specialist nurses, occupational therapists and counsellors. Treatment usually involves an initial outpatient assessment of individual needs. A period of controlled withdrawal from alcohol may be necessary for those patients who are physically dependent. Thereafter, a number of specialist treatments aimed at relapse prevention can be employed, including: counselling; solution focused relapse prevention therapy; cognitive behavioural therapy; stress management; relaxation techniques; group therapy and pharmacotherapy. Many units encourage patients to attend AA meetings, which can be a useful adjunct to other treatments; indeed many units host AA meetings on their premises. Some interventions combine psychological approaches with practical help attending to social needs such as accommodation and employment and developing a supportive social network.

Most patients can be treated as out-patients; if required they can undergo withdrawal from alcohol at home and can then be supported in the community by attending individual or group therapy; attendance for treatment at a day centre may be particularly useful for those patients who need more time to adjust to an abstinent way of life. In common with many medical conditions, such as diabetes, alcohol misuse is best managed with

long-term contact and additional intensive support, if and when problems arise.

In-patient treatment may be necessary for a minority of patients for controlled withdrawal from alcohol and further assessment. This inpatient period may be extended to give patients an opportunity to identify and deal with some of the problems that may be preventing them from effecting change.

In some circumstances, for example, when the patient has no social support or accommodation, more prolonged residential care will be necessary. The homeless problem drinker usually finds it very hard to abstain unless they can be helped out of their 'skid row' surroundings of lodging houses or sleeping rough; hostels therefore play an important role in their rehabilitation.

There are a number of privately run residential services that provide both controlled withdrawal from alcohol and rehabilitation. Many run a relapse prevention service as part of their aftercare programme.

GROUPS WITH SPECIAL NEEDS

Services should be accessible to ALL but some groups may require special consideration, and in some instances, additional specialist services:

Ethnic minority groups may feel particularly stigmatized within their own community because of traditional taboos concerning alcohol or difficulty in approaching conventional services. Awareness of cultural norms and of how these have been breached is valuable when dealing with clients from these communities. Few specific services are available but help may be available from outreach workers from other services.

Young people and particularly adolescents often lack awareness of their problems with alcohol and, more importantly, often do not know how to access help when they finally realise they are in trouble. It is often very difficult for them to engage with traditional health services and hence their presentation may be circuitous or else dramatic. Teachers or youth workers may recognise the signs and consequences of excessive drinking in their adolescent charges or may be told by them, in confidence, about an alcohol problem. Others may present at Accident and Emergency departments with severe intoxication or following an overdose or accident, or may, for similar reasons, come to the attention of the police or social services.

There are relatively few services specifically designed for adolescent problem drinkers. Retaining an adolescent in treatment is often extremely difficult and a good relationship, once established, with an experienced worker is often the key to achieving change. In addition, the needs of young people misusing alcohol should always be considered within the context of their other health and social needs. Most will be dealt with by generalist primary level services; those with more complex problems may be referred to adolescent services but only a minority reach the scarce services designed specifically for children or adolescents with addiction problems.

The coexistence of alcohol and drug misuse is very common at this age and addiction services recognise the need to help the individual move away from relying on alcohol and other drugs as an integral part of their life. This may require avoiding damaging peer group influences, which is very difficult to achieve, and requires skilled help and the provision of satisfying alternatives. The family is often very upset by these behaviours and should be offered appropriate help and advice.

Parents are legally responsible for the care of their children until the age of 18 years. Thus, treatment of a child with an alcohol problem should normally proceed with the full knowledge and involvement of their parents or guardians. However, legislation is clear that the rights of the child are paramount and, in rare cases, where an older child is deemed competent to understand the implications of treatment it may be appropriate to respect their confidences about alcohol misuse. Clinicians working with children need to be familiar with the legal framework of the Children's Act and the priority it gives to the welfare of the child.

Older problem drinkers are often overlooked and their problems neglected. Some may have been misusing alcohol for many years but others may have only started to drink later in life following retirement, bereavement or the onset of failing health. Recognition is the key clinical issue for this age group. Alcohol services should not discriminate on grounds of age and many older people can be effectively helped within existing services. However, there are a number of issues which may make engagement difficult, including, frailty, sleep problems, social isolation, depression, loss of mental acuity and mobility. In addition, the presence of co-morbidities and the use of medication create additional problems which may require specialist input.

The prison population contains many men and women who have severe alcohol problems and this may have been a significant factor in their offending. These individuals should be identified and offered help in avoiding relapse on release. An increasing number of prisons offer programmes designed to help the offender to either drink more sensibly in the future or to abstain. AA is also active in most prisons. Nonetheless these interventions are rarely effective unless combined with a specific through care plan that links the individual with continuing support in the community, once released. Probation officers and social workers play an important part in the rehabilitation of offenders who have serious social problems along with their dependence on alcohol.

LEARNING POINTS

- Individuals drinking at hazardous and harmful levels should be offered help to modify their drinking behaviour.

- The degree of help required does not depend necessarily on the severity of the drinking problem.

- Treatment should be tailored to meet individual's specific needs and might include brief intervention, self-help groups, community-based services, pharmacotherapy and specialist addiction services.

- Many individuals drinking at hazardous levels, and some drinking harmfully, respond well to brief intervention.

- Dependent drinkers usually require a period of controlled withdrawal from alcohol before further engagement with services.

- Acamprosate is the most cost-effective and cost-beneficial of the existing pharmacotherapies.

- Certain vulnerable groups, for example, ethnic minorities, adolescents, the elderly and the prison population pose additional problems for existing services.

CHAPTER 7

THE MANAGEMENT OF SPECIFIC ALCOHOL-RELATED PROBLEMS
-with individual case studies

There are a number of specific problems that arise in individuals misusing alcohol, which require careful and expert management and therefore deserve special mention. Some of these present as tangible, identifiable problems, for example alcohol intoxication and withdrawal and can be managed relatively easily using guidelines and protocols. Others, for example, failure to engage with services, drinking in pregnancy and recidivism are far more complex and are generally managed using the basic principles of good clinical practice in the absence of specific or defined management guidelines. Thus, while the management of the more straight forward problems can be simply narrated the more complex problems are best illustrated using actual case histories.

ALCOHOL INTOXICATION

Clinically apparent intoxication is usually present, in näive drinkers, when blood alcohol concentration reach 150 to 250 mg/100 ml (32.6 to 54.4 mMol/l), while concentrations of 350 mg/100 ml (76 mMol/l) are associated with stupor and coma. Concentrations of > 450 mg/100 ml (98 mMol/l) are often fatal. Individuals who habitually misuse alcohol often develop tolerance to its effects and are significantly less likely to develop intoxication than non-habitual drinkers. In adults, the fatal dose is approximately 5 to 8 g/kg body weight (6 to 10 ml/kg absolute ethanol), although habitual drinkers are able to tolerate higher doses. In children, the fatal dose is lower at approximately 3 g/kg body weight (4 ml/kg absolute ethanol).

The National Poisons Information Service* advises that all children with features of alcohol intoxication should be referred to hospital. Those who have ingested > 0.4 ml/kg body weight of absolute ethanol (i.e. 1 ml/kg of 40% spirit, 4 ml/kg of 10% wine or 8 ml/kg of 5% beer) should be observed for at least 4 hours.

Adults who are mildly to moderately intoxicated can be managed satisfactorily in relatively simple surroundings with a minimum of medical support, while those who are severely intoxicated should be referred to hospital.

The level of consciousness should be assessed at least hourly in anyone admitted with alcohol intoxication; the ECG should be continuously monitored; the urine output must be carefully recorded; blood glucose levels, plasma electrolytes and blood gases should be measured every 4 hours until recovery is assured. Intravenous fluids should be given to counter dehydration and to maintain urine output; plasma expanders may be required if circulatory collapse occurs; inotropic support with dopamine or dobutamine may be necessary if severe hypotension persists. Hypoglycaemia should be corrected as quickly as possible with oral glucose, if the conscious level permits, or else with 5% or 10% IV dextrose as required. Assisted ventilation may be needed if respiration is severely depressed. Haemodialysis may have a place in the management of individuals with exceptionally high blood ethanol concentrations particularly if there are other metabolic complications, evidenced by an arterial pH of < 7, or if the individual has ingested other dialyzable drugs.

*This service, which is accessed *via* www.toxbase.org, is freely available to UK NHS hospitals and general practices, NHS Departments of Public Health and HPA Units. This service is used by NHS Direct and NHS 24 but it is not available to individual members of the public.

Several complications may arise which will need additional skilled management; these include ketoacidosis, lactic acidosis, cardiac arrhythmias, hypokalaemia, inhalation pneumonia, venous thromboembolism and hyperpyrexia. It is important to remember that hypoglycaemia may be delayed for up to 36 hours.

Alternative or additional causes for the changes in conscious level should also be sought particularly in adults with blood alcohol concentrations of <400 mg/100ml (87 mmol/l) who present in coma. Cerebral trauma, cerebrovascular events, meningitis and use of other narcotic or sedative drugs should be excluded.

Metadoxine (pyridoxal L-2-pyrrolidine-5-carboxylate) has been shown to accelerate the elimination of alcohol in adults leading to faster recovery from intoxication. It is given as a single intravenously dose and has few if any side effects. Currently it is not licensed for use in the UK.

ALCOHOL WITHDRAWAL EFFECTS

Approximately 40% of individuals who misuse alcohol will develop an acute withdrawal syndrome when they abruptly stop or substantially reduce their alcohol intake. Most patients manifest a 'minor symptom complex or syndrome', which may start as early as 6 to 8 hours after an abrupt reduction in alcohol intake. It may include any combination of generalized hyperactivity, anxiety, tremor, sweating, nausea, retching, tachycardia, hypertension and mild pyrexia. These symptoms usually peak between 10 to 30 hours and subside by 40 to 50 hours. Fits may occur in the first 12 to 48 hours and only rarely after this. Less frequently, auditory and visual hallucinations arise, which are characteristically frightening, and may last for 5 to 6 days.

Delirium tremens occurs uncommonly, perhaps in less than 5% of individuals withdrawing from alcohol. The syndrome usually starts some 48 to 72 hours after cessation of drinking and is characterized by coarse tremor, agitation, fever, tachycardia, profound confusion, delusions and hallucinations. Convulsions may herald the onset of the syndrome but are not part of the symptom complex. Hyperpyrexia, ketoacidosis and profound circulatory collapse may develop.

Minor degrees of alcohol withdrawal are commonly encountered and individuals can be managed without recourse to specific therapy. However, patients with moderate or severe alcohol withdrawal symptoms should probably be sedated in order to prevent exhaustion and injury; the drugs most commonly used are the benzodiazepines and chlormethiazole. The aim in using these drugs is to control the withdrawal symptoms and to keep the patient comfortable but not over-sedated.

Patients who agree to stop drinking but who do not wish or need to be hospitalized can usually be withdrawn from alcohol as outpatients or at home. Indeed many patients can be managed safely and effectively in this setting supervised by a specialist community nurse. However, certain patients are best withdrawn from alcohol in a hospital setting. These include patients who have experienced severe withdrawal symptoms in the past, have a history of fitting, significant co-morbidities or complex social needs.

Pharmacotherapy may be delivered in one of three ways:

Front-loaded: a single large dose of medication is provided at the start of treatment while subsequent doses are given on an 'as required' basis.

Symptom-triggered: the severity of the patients' withdrawal symptoms and signs are regularly assessed and monitored clinically with or without the help of a designated questionnaire; medication is provided accordingly.

Fixed dose: medication is provided in a standard dose which is then reduced steadily over several days, with the option of 'as required' therapy for breakthrough symptoms.

Overall, symptom-triggered dosing regimens are associated with the use of significantly less medication over a shorter period of time. However, these regimens are resource-intensive and are perhaps best suited for use in specialist centres. The fixed dose regimens can be used in most settings, and indeed are, but of course have the disadvantage that some patients who receive the drugs may not need them.

The benzodiazepines differ little in efficacy from one another but the longer-acting drugs, diazepam and chlordiazepoxide, have the advantage of a smoother more protracted effect, though there is the possibility that their accumulation may cause problems in patients with respiratory or hepatic impairment. The shorter-acting drugs have little tendency to accumulate but the incidence of fitting is higher with these agents. In fixed dose regimens the benzodiazepines, whether short- or long-acting, are given in high dosage on days 1 to 3 and are then tapered over the next 4 to 7 days in response to the patient's condition. Patients' needs are extremely variable and so the dosage of medication is difficult to predict accurately. As a guide, the daily dosages commonly employed in the early phase of treatment might be diazepam 40 mg, chlordiazepoxide 120 mg and lorezepam 8 mg. After the third day, dose reduction of at least 25% daily is required (Table 7.1).

Chlormethiazole should be restricted for use in hospital settings and is usually given as a loading dose of between 2 to 4 capsules, each containing 192 mg chlormethiazole base, followed by administration of between 9 to 12 capsules, in divided doses, over the next 24 hours (Table 7.2). Thereafter, the dose is reduced in a stepwise fashion modified in light of the patient's response. Alternatively, the drug may be dispensed as a syrup containing 250 mg of chlormethiazole edisylate in 5 ml, in a dosage equivalent of 5 ml of syrup to 1 capsule.

Convulsions can be treated with intravenous diazepam in a dose of 0.15 to 0.25 mg/kg body weight (usually 10 to 20 mg) every 4 hours by slow intravenous injection or infusion. Diazemuls (diazepam emulsion injection) is preferred to plain diazepam as it is less likely to cause thrombophlebitis. Lorazepam, given in a dose of 2 to 4 mg (0.7 µg/kg: maximum 4 mg) by rapid bolus injection, is preferred by some physicians as it has more predictable pharmacokinetics and a shorter half-life; however, caution should be exercised in its use if there is any suspicion of underlying liver injury. Hallucinations may require treatment with lorazepam, haloperidol or olanzapine.

Care must be taken to maintain the patient's general condition during the withdrawal period. Dehydration should be corrected, whenever necessary, by use of oral fluids; intravenous fluids should be avoided in hospitalized patients as over hydration is a serious potential hazard. Several biochemical abnormalities may be observed during the withdrawal period such as hypokalaemia and hypomagnesaemia but these are usually transient and do not need specific correction;

TABLE 7.1: Sample fixed dose regimen for treatment of alcohol withdrawal with chlordiazepoxide

Time	Dosage
Day 1, i.e. first 24 hr	30 mg q.d.s.
Day 2	20 mg t.d.s. 30 mg nocte
Day 3	10 mg t.d.s. 20 mg nocte
Day 4	5 mg t.d.s. 10 mg nocte
Day 5	5 mg mane 10 mg nocte
Day 6	5 mg nocte
THEN STOP	

A variable 5 to 10 mg 'p.r.n.' dose can be prescribed for breakthrough symptoms occurring during the withdrawal period.

TABLE 7.2: Sample fixed dose regimen for treatment of alcohol withdrawal with chlormethiazole

Time	Dosage
Initial	2 to 4 capsules
Day 1, i.e. first 24 hr.	9 to 12 capsules in 3/4 doses
Days 2 and 3	6 to 8 capsules in 3/4 doses
Days 4 and 5	4 to 6 capsules in 2/3 doses
Days 6 and 7	Gradually tapered
THEN STOP	

Alternatively, use 5ml syrup = 1 capsule

A variable 1 or 2 capsule 'p.r.n.' dose can be prescribed for breakthrough symptoms occurring during the withdrawal period.

more persistent abnormalities should, of course, be corrected accordingly. The patient should be encouraged to eat a nutritious diet as soon as possible; supplemental feeds may be needed in the first 48 hours if anorexia and nausea are prominent. Vitamin supplementation should be considered (Table 3.5).

Many individuals who have become dependent on alcohol will also have used other drugs, particularly benzodiazepines. These drugs are often prescribed by doctors to help control anxiety symptoms or to effect long-term withdrawal from alcohol. It is often more difficult to withdraw patients from the benzodiazepines, to which they invariably become addicted, than it is to withdraw them from alcohol. In this situation benzodiazepines should be used to withdraw the individual from alcohol but these drugs will then themselves need to be withdrawn over a much more prolonged period.

FITTING

Individuals with a history of established epilepsy may develop fitting if they *acutely* misuse alcohol, independently of their use of anti-epileptic medication. Particular difficulties may arise in individuals on long-term treatment for their epilepsy who *chronically* misuse alcohol because their compliance with medication tends to be poor and because of the unpredictable effects of alcohol on the metabolism of the various anti-epileptic agents; the net effect is often one of unpredictable fitting which is difficult to control. These individuals should clearly be counselled to drink within the recommended guidelines or else, if they have a history of chronic misuse, to remain abstinent from alcohol.

Individuals who misuse alcohol may develop fitting when intoxicated. The fits should be brought under control with parenteral benzodiazepines but with great care as the blood ethanol concentration may still be significantly elevated. An EEG should be undertaken in all individuals experiencing this type of fitting, for the first time, together with some form of cerebral imaging, either CT or MRI, in order to exclude potential underlying pathology. These individuals should be counselled about their drinking behaviour, as the fits are likely to recur during further episodes of intoxication. *There is no indication for use of prophylactic anti-epileptic medication in this setting.*

Fitting may also develop in alcohol dependent individuals when they withdraw from alcohol. The fits are managed with

benzodiazepines. Again an EEG should be undertaken in all individuals developing this type of fitting for the first time together with cerebral CT or MRI imaging, if further indicated. Likewise they should be counselled about their drinking behaviour and warned that the fitting will most likely recur if they continue to misuse alcohol and experience further episodes of withdrawal. Again *there is no indication for use of prophylactic anti-epileptic medication in this setting.*

Individuals who chronically misuse alcohol may suffer head trauma and develop cerebral injury or subdural or extradural haematomas. These injuries may result in the development of fitting, either at the time of the initial insult, or subsequently. These individuals are extremely difficult to manage. They may require long-term, anti-epileptic medication but if they continue to misuse alcohol then control may be difficult, if not impossible, to achieve.

Approximately 10% of chronic alcohol misusers develop late-onset epilepsy in the absence of focal cerebral lesions. These individuals require anti-epileptic medication and are also difficult to manage but can do relatively well if they abstain from alcohol long-term.

ANAESTHESIA

The anaesthetist called upon to deal with an intoxicated patient faces several problems. It is unlikely that a drinking history will be available from the patient, thus it will be difficult to assess tolerance to alcohol and hence cross-tolerance to drugs. Equally, little or no information will be available on the state of their liver and thus it will be difficult to gauge the likelihood of cross-reactions with the various anaesthetic dugs likely to be used. It is clearly important, therefore, to try to obtain a history of the patient's drinking habits from a relative or friend stressing the clinical need for accurate information. In addition, general anaesthesia should be avoided if at all possible; regional anaesthesia with response-titrated sedation is the safest option. However, if general anaesthesia can not be avoided then a number of factors will have to be taken into account.

It is relatively easy to anaesthetize an intoxicated näive drinker since basal 'narcosis' already exists; in consequence, less anaesthetic agent may be required. However, alcohol may compound or potentiate the effects of a number of the drugs used to induce and maintain anaesthesia or to procure post-operative sedation and analgesia.

Acutely intoxicated individuals may have sizeable gastric residues and this will increase the risk of regurgitation and aspiration during induction. Steps should, therefore, be taken to empty the stomach before the patient is anaesthetized.

Habitual drinkers who have developed metabolic tolerance to alcohol are likely to display cross-tolerance to a number of drugs used in anaesthetic practice. Modest increases in the dosage of a variety of intravenous induction agents may, therefore, be necessary. The response to the inhalation agents used for induction is less predictable; some patients will display severe excitement while others become anaesthetized more readily; in consequence these agents are best avoided.

Autonomic circulatory reflexes may be impaired in these individuals with the result that they may not develop warning signs of impending shock such as tachycardia and sweating. The anaesthetist may not, therefore, realise that anything is amiss until the patient suddenly becomes hypotensive and collapses.

Chronic alcohol misuse is associated with the development of cardiomyopathy, which is often subclinical; the presence of flattened T waves on the ECG together with atrial arrhythmias is suggestive. In these circumstances anaesthetic agents such as halothane, which increase myocardial irritability, are best avoided as they might precipitate dangerous arrhythmias.

Hypoglycaemia may develop rapidly during anaesthesia especially in individuals drinking heavily prior to admission to hospital. Hypoglycaemia is particularly difficult to recognise in anaesthetized patients; blood sugar levels should, therefore, be monitored carefully throughout.

Habitual heavy drinkers are often heavy smokers and so may have chronic obstructive airways disease. In addition, the presence of cirrhosis may be complicated by the development of intrapulmonary arteriovenous shunting of blood. Thus, hypoxia may develop during anaesthesia and this might, in turn, precipitate hepatic failure.

Patients with chronic liver disease avidly retain sodium although their serum sodium concentrations may be normal or low reflecting the presence of fluid retention; infusion of saline solutions should be avoided, if at all possible, because of the danger of precipitating pulmonary oedema. These patients may also be hypokalaemic because of a reduction in total body potassium stores. Every effort should be made to increase circulating potassium concentrations before anaesthesia, especially if there are associated ECG changes, such as S-T segment depression and T-wave inversion.

POST-OPERATIVE CARE

Problem drinkers can be unco-operative, irrational and aggressive and their behaviour may deteriorate further in the post-operative period if they develop acute withdrawal symptoms. This situation is difficult to manage as vital drips, tubes and drains need to be preserved and because the situation often develops at night when nursing and medical staff may be in short supply. The patient obviously needs sedation but it is difficult to know how this should be achieved; problem drinkers with little or no liver disease are often extremely resistant to the effects of opiates and sedatives while their counterparts with significant liver injury may show extreme cerebral sensitivity to these agents such that even small doses may precipitate hepatic encephalopathy. A slow infusion of a relatively short-acting benzodiazepine, which is response-titrated, provides the best and safest option. However, it is also important to ensure that the patients receive effective pain relief and this is best effected by use of a response-titrated infusion of a short-acting opiate.

Wound healing tends to be poor and abdominal wound dehiscence is particularly likely to occur in problem drinkers especially those with significant liver injury who develop ascites in the post-operative period. Such patients are also prone to intra-operative and post-operative bleeding because of their multiple clotting abnormalities. Opportunistic infections are common and are easily overlooked at this time.

DRUG INTERACTIONS

The interplay between drugs and the acute and chronic effects of alcohol is both extensive and complex. In addition, the presence of liver disease may significantly affect drug handling. Extra care must, therefore, be exercised when prescribing drugs for individuals who have just consumed alcohol, or for those who habitually misuse alcohol.

EFFECTS OF ACUTE ALCOHOL INGESTION

Inhibition: Alcohol may directly inhibit the action of several drugs as a result of:

- competitive inhibition;
- displacement of the drug from cytochrome P450 sites;
- release of competitive inhibitors of drug metabolizing enzymes;
- depression of NADPH by impairment of the citric acid cycle;
- disruption of lipid membranes.

Thus, the metabolism of drugs normally occupying the microsomal system, such as phenytoin, barbiturates and anticoagulants will be impaired in the presence of high circulating levels of alcohol, and their dosage will require modification accordingly. The use of such drugs in individuals who chronically misuse alcohol is clearly fraught with danger; alcohol misuse is, therefore, a relative contraindication to their use.

Additive effects: The actions of certain drugs may be increased by an effect of alcohol itself. Thus, individuals with diabetes who drink alcohol regularly are more likely to develop hypoglycaemia when treated with sulphonylureas or to develop lactic acidosis when treated with biguanides.

Potentiation: Alcohol may enhance the action of certain drugs; the distinction between additive and potentiating effects is sometimes difficult to make, but is of little practical consequence. Equally, certain drugs may enhance the actions of alcohol. Cerebral depression occurs more readily when alcohol is used with sedatives and narcotics, but also with antihistamines, antitussives, anticonvulsants and analgesics. Drowsiness, ataxia, impaired judgement and even coma may result. Similarly, if alcohol is taken with vasodilator drugs, flushing may be more noticeable, while patients taking antihypertensive agents may develop profound hypotension if they consume alcohol. Tricyclic antidepressants further compound the effects of alcohol on motor skills, while alcohol increases the inhibitory effects of tricyclics on gastrointestinal motility.

Specific metabolic interactions: The best example of a specific metabolic interaction between alcohol and a drug is the inhibition of ADH activity by disulfiram (Antabuse). If patients taking this drug consume alcohol,

acetaldehyde rapidly accumulates in the blood, and within 5 to 15 minutes they develop flushing, tachycardia, headache, vomiting and dyspnoea; severe hypotension, collapse and even death may ensue.

A number of other drugs may exhibit a mild 'Antabuse-like' effect including:

- chloramphenicol, metronidazole, ß-lactam antibiotics, griseofulvin;
- procarbazine;
- sulphonylureas such as chlorpropamide and tolbutamide; the specific 'flushing reaction' sometimes seen with chlorpropamide is a related phenomenon.

Enhancement of toxicity: Alcohol appears to increase the gastric mucosal irritant action of salicylates and other non-steroidal, anti-inflammatory drugs. The combination of alcohol with aspirin appears to increase the risk of gastrointestinal haemorrhage as alcohol potentiates the coagulation defect induced by this drug.

Alcohol may also increase the severity of some adverse hepatic drug reactions, for example, methotrexate injury. Likewise individuals who drink regularly may development paracetamol-related liver injury following ingestion of much lower doses of this drug than ordinarily associated with toxicity.

EFFECTS OF CHRONIC ALCOHOL MISUSE

Chronic alcohol misuse is associated with the induction of hepatic enzymes and progressive hepatic damage; both of these factors can alter the way in which drugs are handled by the liver.

Enzyme induction: Individuals who misuse alcohol tend to 'hold their drink well'. Tolerance develops, in part because of central nervous system adaptation, but also because the ability to metabolize alcohol increases in alcohol misusers following induction of the MEOS system. This oxidizing system is shared with a number of drugs such as warfarin, tolbutamide and phenytoin whose elimination rates may, therefore, increase in habitual drinkers. Thus, the amount of drug required to produce a therapeutic effect in individuals misusing alcohol may increase, only to fall rapidly when drinking ceases.

Liver injury: Advanced liver disease is associated with impairment of the metabolism not only of alcohol itself but also of drugs that are dependent on hepatic metabolism for their elimination. Individuals with cirrhosis may be hypoalbuminaemic and this will affect the distribution and penetration of protein-bound drugs, such as, corticosteroids. In addition the sensitivity of the brain to certain centrally-acting drugs is increased in patients with chronic liver disease.

ADDITIONAL PROBLEMS

Inappropriate responses: Problem drinkers frequently display unexpected responses to drugs, for example, to anaesthetic agents, which are difficult to explain on the basis of current knowledge and which are hard to predict.

Poor compliance: Alcohol misusers are notorious for their poor compliance with treatment. They often lack motivation and this may be aggravated by the development of brain damage. Penury, neglect and social disturbance all contribute to the difficulties encountered in treating these individuals.

Gastrointestinal intolerance: Problem drinkers often suffer from anorexia, nausea and vomiting and this interferes with drug ingestion and absorption.

Congener effects: Additives and congeners in some beverages may occasionally affect drug handling. Thus, the tyramine found in some wines and beers may react with monoamine oxidase inhibitors to produce a severe hypertensive reaction.

AGGRESSIVE PATIENTS

Although most intoxicated patients are cooperative and accept help and advice some may be belligerent, abusive and violent. The overriding priority in this situation is to ensure the patient's safety and that of attending staff, relatives/friends and bystanders. It is equally important to try to assess whether the patient is angry and disinhibited simply because they are intoxicated or because other factor such as injury or infection have added a component of confusion or delirium.

Every attempt should be made to create a calm environment. Those not immediately concerned with the patient's management should be asked to leave. Ensure that the room is clear of objects that can be thrown or used as a weapon and ensure that your own exit is not impeded.

It is often possible to defuse escalating anger by adopting a non-judgemental, concerned manner and a non-threatening demeanour. There is little point in arguing with someone who is very drunk.

Many hospitals have security staff and police on standby and it is important to ensure that they can be summoned promptly so that help is immediately to hand. Their intervention is rarely necessary but their presence is important as it conveys a clear message that violence will not be tolerated.

If felt appropriate the patient should be offered 'something to calm them down', but sedatives should always be used sparingly in this situation because of the danger of over sedation and masking of other conditions that might be affecting cerebral function. If the patient refuses help and their aggression continues to escalate it is probably better to try to isolate them in as safe an environment as possible rather than to try to forcibly restrain and sedate them. However, restraint is sometimes necessary but should always be carried out by staff trained in the correct procedures and should always be viewed as an option of last resort. The drug of choice in this situation would be haloperidol. If the patient is sedated then they will need to be carefully monitored over the next several hours. This is particularly important in individuals who are dependent drinkers because at some stage they may develop features of alcohol withdrawal.

If someone is mentally ill, confused, disorientated, suicidal or significantly depressed, detention under the Mental Health Act may be needed but this is not justified in most cases of intoxication and aggressive behaviour. It is wise to involve a psychiatric colleague before detaining someone in this way.

Patients may have no subsequent memory of the events that took place when they were intoxicated. Thus, when staff relate these events and show them the damage they have caused they may not respond with the contrition expected. A collateral report from a family member or friend often has more effect. Equally any advice given to patients in their intoxicated state will not be retained and it is incumbent on staff to provide information on sources of help in writing and if possible to pass the patient into the care of a responsible relative or friend who should also be aware of the advice given and of any follow-up arrangements made.

LEARNING POINTS

Alcohol Intoxication

- Adults who are severely intoxicated and all children with features of alcohol intoxication should be referred to hospital.

- Patients with acute intoxication should be closely observed for evidence of respiratory depression.

- Alternative causes of impaired consciousness should be sought in adults with blood alcohol levels below 400 mg/100 ml.

Alcohol Withdrawal

- Approximately 40% of alcohol misusers develop an acute withdrawal syndrome when they abruptly stop or substantially reduce their alcohol intake; in the majority these are mild to moderate in severity.

- The majority of dependent individuals can be withdrawn from alcohol as outpatients or at home; those who have previously experienced severe withdrawal symptoms, have a history of fitting, significant co-morbidities or complex social needs are best hospitalized.

- The drugs most commonly used for alcohol withdrawal are the benzodiazepines.

Fitting

- Fitting is associated with both alcohol intoxication and alcohol withdrawal and is best managed with benzodiazepines; these individuals should not be given prophylactic anti-epileptic medication.

Anaesthesia & Post-Operative Care

- Alcohol may compound or potentiate the effects of a number of drugs used to induce and maintain anaesthesia and those used for post-operative sedation and analgesia.

- General anaesthesia should be avoided in individuals who are acutely intoxicated and only undertaken after careful consideration in habitual drinkers. Regional anaesthesia with carefully monitored sedation is safer.

- Post-operative alcohol withdrawal is best managed with a response-titrated, slow infusion of a short-acting benzodiazepine; analgesia is best provided with a short-acting opiate infusion.

Drug Interactions

- Alcohol, whether taken acutely or chronically, can significantly affect the handling of many drugs particularly, though not exclusively, those metabolized *via* the MEOS system.

- The interplay between drugs and alcohol is often unpredictable and prescribers should avoid medication in individuals with a history of alcohol misuse, whenever possible.

Aggression

- Aggressive, intoxicated individual should be assessed, if possible, to identify factors such as injury or infection which might confound the clinical picture.

- The safety of the patient and of the attendant staff is of paramount importance and governs the management approach.

ILLUSTRATIVE CASE HISTORIES

1. The Pregnant Drinker

A young Polish woman came to England to take up a job as a hairdresser in her cousin's saloon. She was 24 weeks pregnant at the time and had received no previous antenatal care. She registered with a local general practitioner who, concerned that the baby was small for dates, referred her for an urgent antenatal assessment. The midwife who saw her thought she smelt of alcohol but excess consumption was denied. The ultrasound scan confirmed that the baby was small for dates and she was recalled. She was devastated that there was 'something wrong' with the baby and agreed to be admitted to hospital for bed rest and more detailed investigation. When questioned further she admitted that although she had been abstinent for the first three months of her pregnancy she had been drinking ever since but 'socially.' She denied that she had an alcohol problem and resisted further enquiry.

She remained well for the first day after admission and engaged with the other women on the ward. However, she became very restless during her second night in hospital getting up frequently and wandering the corridors. By the following morning she was sweating and tremulous but there was no evidence of infection and no obvious obstetric cause for her distress. The medical registrar on call was asked to see her urgently and as he approached the bed she began to fit. He had very little information about her but was able to ascertain that there were no features suggestive of pre-eclampsia. He gave her a small dose of a short-acting benzodiazepine intravenously and the fitting fairly rapidly came under control. She was transferred to a medical ward where a more detailed alcohol history was obtained and her withdrawal was managed successfully with a short-acting benzodiazepine over the next 5 days with additional close monitoring by the obstetrics team. Benzodiazepines are potentially teratogenic but her pregnancy was fairly well advanced and the benefits to her and to the baby of reducing the risk of further fitting considerably outweighed the risks to the baby from the drug.

Her relatives, who had been unaware of her pregnancy until she had arrived in the country, were supportive and with help from the hospital alcohol liaison service she was able to maintain abstinence until she was delivered prematurely of a baby girl at 36 weeks. The baby was small but showed no obvious signs of fetal alcohol effects disorder and no major congenital abnormalities. The baby spent 7 days in the neonatal unit under observation and was then allowed home with her mother. The health visitor was aware of the background and both mother and baby were carefully monitored. Concerns were raised by her relatives when the baby was 2 months old that the mother was drinking again but at this stage she decided to no longer engage with services and suddenly returned to Poland. The relatives promised that they would make sure that the baby's grandparents were aware of the problems there had been in England to ensure that she, at least, would be adequately followed-up in the longer term.

LEARNING POINTS

- All women should have a drinking history taken at first antenatal contact.

- Women who have received little or no antenatal care in early pregnancy should be carefully screened for alcohol-related problem when they eventually present.

- Alcohol withdrawal in pregnancy requires careful management with cooperation between obstetricians, physicians and alcohol liaison services.

- Women who have been drinking during pregnancy are particularly vulnerable in the postnatal period.

- Children of mothers who misuse alcohol during pregnancy need careful long-term follow-up.

2. The Worried Relative

Dear Dr. Jones,

I find this a very difficult letter to write because I feel I am being very disloyal to my father but I don't know what else to do. I know he is a patient of yours and I know that you have been concerned about his drinking. He's probably told you that everything's fine and that he isn't drinking anymore but this just isn't true. He's drinking every night after work, and at weekends he drinks all the time. My mother has tried to reason with him, particularly as she knows how concerned you have been about his health, especially his blood pressure, but he just doesn't listen. Worst of all I found out last weekend, when I came home from University, that he has been hitting her. She won't tell anyone about this and she would be terribly upset if she knew I was writing to you as she is a very private person but I just don't know what else to do. I daren't tell my brother as they have already fallen out and he would probably kill my father if he knew he was hurting my mother. I have begged my mother to come and stay with me in Leicester but she doesn't want to leave my father on his own and my boyfriend is upset as he feels I shouldn't get involved. Please could you see my father and try to make him see reason as otherwise I am worried that something serious will happen but PLEASE don't mention I have written to you as my mother would never forgive me.

Yours sincerely

The Doctor's Response:

Mr Y is well known to me. He is a successful businessman. He is married with a daughter who is at university, of whom he is very proud, and a son who initially worked in the family business but following a major falling out moved away to set up his own.

Mr Y has contacted me on a number of occasions in the last 18 months about gastrointestinal upsets and admitted fairly early on that he was drinking 'a little too much'. His face was very florid; he was significantly hypertensive and had a raised serum GTT. He acknowledged, after some persuasion, that he was very worried about his drinking but was confident that he could bring it under control. He did not feel the need for outside help.

Initially he decided he would reduce his intake to recommended levels but his blood pressure was difficult to control with medication and his serum GGT remained high. Approximately 6 months ago it was agreed that the best course of action for him would be to abstain from alcohol completely, and this he appears to have done. He reports abstinence, his blood pressure is better controlled and his serum GGT, although still abnormal, has improved. However, he continues to have 'abdominal problems' and appears anxious but he attributes this to ongoing worries about his business.

His wife is also a patient of mine but neither of the children is registered with the practice. Clearly I cannot divulge the information the daughter has provided but equally I can not ignore it, particularly as Mrs Y is also my patient.

I wrote to the daughter to explain that the rules of patient confidentiality preclude me from revealing anything about her father's condition but also to express my concern about the ongoing difficulties she reported. I suggested that she try to persuade her mother to make an appointment to see me when I would endeavour to get her to talk about her concerns. Alternatively she and her mother could contact one of the support organisations for relatives of problem drinkers such as AlAnon where they would receive support and advice. I also emphasized that if she had real concerns about her mother's safety she should persuade her to contact the local Domestic Violence Unit where she could discuss her problems in complete confidence. Equally, if at any time she were fearful for her mother's safety she could contact the Domestic Violence Unit herself.

After I had responded to the daughter's letter I contacted Mr Y and asked him to attend for follow-up blood tests. I explained that the results were concerning as with 6 months abstinence from alcohol they should have retuned to normal. I asked him directly if he were continuing to drink and he reluctantly admitted that this was the case. I suggested that he return, together with his wife, so we could discuss the situation in more details. This he eventually did after a delay of some weeks and his wife was at last able to talk frankly about the situation. He finally accepted the need to change and after a distinctly difficult few months is now, at last, abstinent from alcohol.

LEARNING POINTS

- Many people find it hard to confront a friend or relative about their drinking and this oblique approach for help is common.

- It is useful to involve family or friends in treatment, from the outset, in order to help with behavioural change but also to obtain collateral information on drinking behaviour.

- Health professionals have to respect patient confidentiality but can often use collateral information, even if provided in confidence, to progress treatment.

3. The Drinking Mother

Ms RB was referred for urgent assessment. Little information was provided in the letter from her general practitioner except that she was 41 years old, was jaundiced and had a long history of alcohol misuse and depression. Her background, as it unfolded during her outpatient appointment, was that she had always 'liked a drink' but that her intake had escalated in recent years in response to a number of devastating life events. She had worked as an actuary in a city insurance company from the age of 32 but had been constructively dismissed some 2 years previously. She had attended various tribunals and her allegations were upheld but for some reason she was now involved in proceedings against her former employer and had had to realise most of her assets to do so. Her partner, dismayed at the effect this was having not only on their finances, but also on her physical health – she had dropped from 90 to 43 kg in weight – had left some 8 months previously leaving her in sole charge of their two children, aged 3 and 5, and her 21-year-old disabled son from an earlier, failed marriage.

She was intoxicated, severely malnourished and could barely walk. She had an advanced sensory peripheral neuropathy affecting all four limbs, evidence of cerebellar dysfunction and of significant liver disease. Her laboratory test results were seriously deranged. Her clinical condition was deemed critical and she was offered immediate admission which she refused as she had no one to look after her children. Attempts to convince her that arrangements could be made to take care of her children failed. She was told that if she insisted on going home her general practitioner, who according to her was aware of her family situation, the hospital child protection officer and her local social services would be contacted to ensure that the needs of her children were urgently assessed. She appeared to think that nothing would be found amiss as 'she was a good mother' and 'her children came first.' She was seen that evening by the alcohol liaison team, prescribed supplemental feeds and vitamins, and several investigations organised.

The child protection team and social services visited her at home the next day. They ascertained that although Ms RB had no family support in this country both her ex-partners were willing to help with the children in the short to medium term. Ms RB refused to accept their help until she was told that the only other option was for the children to be taken into care and fostered. The two younger children were collected by their father; he lived locally and arrangements were made for him to receive ongoing support with their care. The care of the older boy was more problematic because of his disabilities and because his father lived 80 miles away. However, social services were able to obtain a placement for him in a residential facility for young disabled people near his father's home, as an interim measure.

LEARNING POINTS

- Health-care professionals must take responsibility for their patients and not simply refer onwards.

- The health and safety of other family members is of equal and, in the case of vulnerable children, greater importance that that of the affected patient.

- Even the most desperate and dysfunctional of situations can be improved if agencies work together.

Ms RB was admitted to a residential facility for medically assisted withdrawal from alcohol once the child care arrangements were in place. She completed a four week programme and although her physical condition was still a cause for concern her mental state had improved considerably. She was offered a place on an aftercare programme but decided that she would instead return to her family home in Nigeria for two to three months as she was sure that 'there would be no chance that anyone would let her drink.' Her plans were then to return to the UK and re-establish her family unit. The children remain with their fathers.

4. The Colluding Family

Mr PP, a 36 year old Sikh man, was transferred to a tertiary liver centre, from another hospital following a substantial bleed from oesophageal varices. He had been drinking heavily from his teens but this was his first presentation. He lived at home with his mother and two sisters; his father, who had drunk heavily but socially, had died some years earlier. The patient had worked as a freelance IT consultant until recently.

His hospital course was stormy; he had several further gastrointestinal bleeds, developed increasing jaundice, fluid retention and fluctuating mental change. He was finally discharged some 8 weeks after admission. The patient and his family were left in no doubt that he was a very sick man and that his best chance of survival was to remain abstinent from alcohol for the rest of his life. This they all appeared to understand and accept. They were linked into both local and hospital-based support services.

Two weeks after discharge he was admitted to his local hospital with a further varicial bleed but did not require transfer. Shortly after his discharge from the local hospital he was reviewed in the outpatient clinic in the tertiary centre; he was acompanied by his family. He claimed that he had been abstinent from alcohol since his initial hospitalization. His laboratory test results were stable and there was no objective evidence that he was still drinking. Nevertheless, he was told quite clearly that his liver was severely damaged and that unless he maintained total abstinence from alcohol it was unlikely that he would survive another year. A week later he was admitted locally with a further varicial bleed and on this occasion his management was complicated by the development of severe alcohol withdrawal, including fitting.

He was reviewed at the tertiary centre two weeks after discharge from the local hospital; he was again accompanied by his mother and sisters. During the consultation the patient admitted that he had been drinking. His sister, when asked, said that she thought he 'was doing well' as he was only drinking in the evenings. It also transpired that his family were buying the alcohol for him as he was 'often too tired to leave the house'. When told that this was not helping the situation his mother replied 'this is what he wants so what can we do.'

Attempts were made to engage the family with an alcohol support group within the Sikh community and initially the situation improved but he was then lost to follow-up by hospital services. Ten months later the general practitioner wrote to say that Mr PP had died following a further gastrointestinal bleed. The sister later wrote to the hospital to say that the family had no idea that their brother was so sick and that they wish they had been told so that they could have helped him more.

LEARNING POINTS

- Relatives often collude because it is sometimes easier to do so.

- Ethnic and cultural factors, which might dictate families responses in these circumstances should be appreciated and taken into account.

- Best endeavours may still fail and this should not be taken personally; it is still possible to learn from these difficult situations.

5. The Errant Student

Mr JJ, a second year medical student, was arrested and reprimanded by the police following an incident during 'Rag week' when part of the College gardens was decimated and a member of the security staff verbally abused. However, this event did not come to the attention of the College authorities. He passed his end of year examinations without difficulty and his performance during his first clinical year, when he was ranked in the second quartile, caused no concerns. He successfully applied for a place on an intercalated BSc in Primary Health Care at another institution.

No problems were apparent until the second term of his iBSc year when he was reprimanded for arriving late for GP surgeries and tutorials. Although his attendance improved his interest and commitment to the course noticeably waned. He was awarded a 2:2 degree; the course director commented that this was a disappointing result given his obvious intelligence and ability.

He returned to his own medical school for his second clinical year which was marred by frequent absences, an incident when the validity of the sign-off signatures in his obstetrics and gynaecology course book was queried but not followed up, and a ranking in the fourth quartile in the end of year examinations.

In November of his final year he was involved in a drunken brawl in the student's bar which came to the attention of his personal tutor. He was referred to the Occupational Health Service but was believed when he said that he did not drink heavily as a rule but had done so on the night in question because his girlfriend had just finished with him. Fortunately they had subsequently sorted out their differences and he had learnt his lesson. He was given a drinks diary and told to keep a record of his drinking behaviour and to report back if 'it was getting out of hand.' He was also provided with details of the student's counselling service and various local help and advice services.

In the February of his final year his personal tutor was contacted, as are all personal or academic tutors, for confirmation that there was no bar to Mr JJ sitting his final examinations. The tutor mentioned the 'bar incident' on the form provided but stipulated that it had been resolved. This was reviewed by the Faculty Welfare Panel and no further action was taken although the tutor was reminded that he should have informed the welfare panel when the event arose. Mr JJ was required to fill in the Transfer of Information form for the Foundation School around the same time. He chose not to declare the incident in his second year as it had never been on the College's radar screen. He subsequently sat and passed his final MB in July of the same year.

When Dr JJ was two months into his FY1 job the head of the Trust's Human Resources alerted his consultant to the fact that the routine Criminal Record Bureau check had shown that he had an undeclared reprimand. He was immediately suspended from duty by the Trust and the GMC was informed. They identified issues of both probity and health and proceeded accordingly. He was eventually required to attend a Fitness to Practice hearing, supported by a solicitor from his defence union. He agreed to accept written undertakings and medical supervision by a GMC nominee to address his problems with alcohol. He was eventually allowed to return to his job under a Trust imposed close supervisory order. His future remains uncertain.

USEFUL WEB-LINKS
Fitness to Practise: http://www.ucl.ac.uk/medicalschool/staff-students/general-information/a-z/#fitness_practise
CRB: http://www.ucl.ac.uk/medicalschool/staff-students/general-information/a-z/#criminal
Transfer of Information: http://www.ucl.ac.uk/medicalschool/careers/ factsheets/Factsheet_4.pdf
Close Supervision: http://www.ucl.ac.uk/medicalschool/staff-students/general-information/a-z/#close
Student Agreement: http://www.ucl.ac.uk/medicalschool/staff-students/UCL_Phase_2_Student_Agreement_0910

CHAPTER 8

THE PREVENTION OF ALCOHOL-RELATED HARM

It is important when attempting to prevent alcohol-related harm to strike a balance between unfettered promotion of drinking and overly restrictive controls. There is a need for a coherent alcohol strategy at both local and national levels. At present there are many examples of policies pulling in different directions, for example, a concern with improving community safety versus the decision to promote all day drinking in the interests of tourism. It is also evident that the impact of alcohol needs to be viewed along with other social and environmental factors that impinge on public health and well-being in general.

PRIMARY PREVENTION

There is good evidence that within any population the level of alcohol consumption is closely linked to availability and cost in relation to disposable income. The 'real' price of alcohol, if account is taken of inflation, has declined steadily in recent decades (Figure 2.4). Regular access to drinking and pressures to drink from advertising and other inducements, such as 'happy hours' or special low cost promotions, encourage increased drinking. Efforts at *primary prevention* should, therefore, focus on reducing both average *per capita* consumption and damaging patterns of drinking, particularly binge drinking amongst young people. The principal measures adopted are:

- Control of availability; i.e. price and licensing policy;
- Public education about sensible use;
- Decrease the incentives to drink;
- Provide alternative leisure activities and non-alcoholic beverages at low cost.

CONTROL OF AVAILABILITY

Controls usually take the form of either taxation or legislation aimed at reducing availability. Such legislation might include raising the permitted age of purchase, restricting the times of sales and/or the number and location of licensed premises, and restricting the density of public houses and off-licence premises. A high density of licensed outlets in a given area increases competition, which promotes special inducements to purchase such as promotional pricing; this undoubtedly contributes to the well-known problems of violence and other disturbances in the inner cities. Controls are often unpopular politically but are amongst the most effective ways of reducing the overall level of alcohol-related harm in the population (Figure 8.1). Surveys show that the public accepts the need to restrict access to alcohol and appreciates the harm caused by unfettered promotions.

In recent years there has been a significant increase in drinking at home because alcohol purchased at off-licence premises, principally in supermarkets, has become so much cheaper than similar drinks bought in on-licence premises such as public houses and restaurants. Some major supermarkets have promoted deep discounting or below cost selling; in these instances alcohol sales are used as a loss leader to encourage the overall sale of goods. Because of the high volume sales they achieve major retailers can also absorb some increase in taxation. In order to counter this and deep discounting promotions, public health interests have advocated setting a minimum price limit per unit of alcohol. Raising the price of the cheapest alcoholic drinks appears to have a greater impact on consumption than raising prices at the more expensive end of the market.

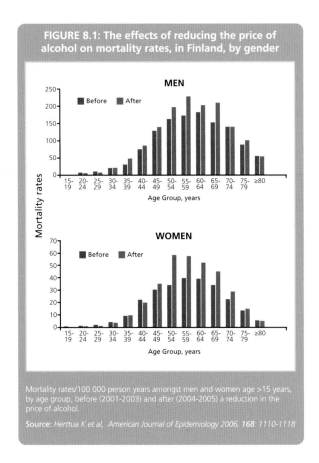

FIGURE 8.1: The effects of reducing the price of alcohol on mortality rates, in Finland, by gender

Mortality rates/100 000 person years amongst men and women age >15 years, by age group, before (2001-2003) and after (2004-2005) a reduction in the price of alcohol.

Source: *Herttua K et al, American Journal of Epidemiology 2006, 168: 1110-1118*

EDUCATION AND HEALTH PROMOTION

Little is known about the best means of influencing drinking cultures. The effects of education and health promotion on alcohol consumption are difficult to demonstrate. In general, the effects of educational campaigns have been disappointing in that while they may increase knowledge of the potential hazards of excess alcohol consumption, they usually have little or no effect on drinking behaviour. Public education about the unit system for measuring alcohol consumption, and the patterns and levels of consumption that are likely to cause harm, are generally useful but again there is no evidence that they produce behavioural change or promote more sensible drinking. More focused education on topics such as drinking and driving or minimising drinking during pregnancy are more effective. Programmes aimed at improving

professionals' understanding of alcohol problems and their willingness to help their patients deal with their drinking problems have also proven effective.

In recent years, educational programmes have been devised to broaden information about all aspects of health, not just the effects of alcohol. These aim to inculcate individuals with a sense of responsibility for their own health and safety and that of the community. They are designed, for example, to assist individuals to decide whether to drink, under what circumstances, and in what quantities, clear in the knowledge of the consequences of their actions, and to resist peer pressures to drink inappropriately. It remains to be seen whether this new approach will be more effective in bringing about change. Peer group education, preferably also involving parents, seems more effective in influencing young people than outside experts lecturing about alcohol use, or other didactic approaches.

CULTURAL CHANGE

Society imposes its own subtle controls on drinking behaviour which are difficult to identify and even more difficult to quantify. In recent years, for example, attitudes to drinking and driving have changed dramatically and individuals who indulge in this sort of behaviour are now considered socially unacceptable. This change in attitude has occurred gradually over time and cannot be attributed to any specific event or series of events. Whether social attitudes to other aspects of excessive or irresponsible drinking will change over time, and influence behaviour, remains to be seen.

Every year, the 'drinks' industry spends vast amounts of money advertising or promoting their wares *via* sponsorship of sporting and cultural activities. In recent years, however, they have been involved with Government in establishing an ethical code of conduct in relation to advertising and sales promotion, and a number of voluntary 'watchdog' organizations are involved in monitoring performance to ensure conformity to the agreed regulations and codes. Some doubt exist, however, as to whether self-monitoring of this kind can ever be truly effective.

Attempts have been made to ensure that advertising does not target teenagers and to enforce, more effectively, laws prohibiting sales to underage drinkers. From a public health and clinical perspective, it is noteworthy that the early onset of drinking correlates closely, not only with subsequent hazardous drinking, but also with smoking and other forms of drug misuse.

SERVER TRAINING AND RESPONSIBILITY

Those who dispense alcohol in bars and restaurants and indeed in their own homes have a responsibility to their customers/guests. There has been increasing interest in training bar staff in responsible serving procedures and in ensuring that they do not serve those who are under age or overtly intoxicated. There has been a particular interest in the server's legal responsibility for allowing someone to drive after drinking. Training schemes for bar staff and managers of public houses are now available and have become a mandatory requirement for licence tenure in many places.

COMMUNITY ACTION

Many communities are now examining the part they can play in reducing alcohol-related harm at a local level, for instance by encouraging alternatives such as non-alcoholic drinks and by not linking social and sporting activities closely with drinking. In some cities new bye-laws have been introduced creating zones in which public drinking is prohibited and attempts have been made to reduce the level of drinking at sporting events by banning alcohol sales before and during the game. Local communities can also help by monitoring the standards of licensed premises and the effects of alcohol misuse on community safety. It is important that health interests are represented in local decisions about alcohol policy and particularly licensing.

SECONDARY PREVENTION

Efforts at *secondary prevention* are usually directed at high-risk groups and are aimed at early diagnosis and intervention. High-risk groups include individuals who consume amounts of alcohol known to be harmful and individuals who, for a variety of genetic, social or constitutional reasons, appear to be either unduly susceptible or else are unduly exposed to the effects of alcohol, for example, women, the young, and those in occupations which allow them free or easy access to alcohol. As the risk of developing alcohol-related physical harm increases significantly with daily intakes of alcohol in excess of 20 g (2.5 units) in women and 40 g (5 units) in men, large proportions of the adult population, in many countries, fall into these high-risk categories. Therefore, the efforts of secondary prevention, in this context, largely overlap with those of primary prevention.

GENERAL POPULATION CAMPAIGNS

A number of campaigns have been undertaken, for example, National Drinkwise Days, designed to increase awareness, among the public at large and amongst individuals in high-risk groups, of the levels of alcohol consumption associated with the development of physical harm and the hazards of binge drinking. Drink-drive campaigns around Christmas and summer holiday periods, combined with greater police activity at these times, are believed to be effective in increasing awareness and reducing offending. These are repeated at intervals and certainly increase awareness and knowledge, but the effects on drinking behaviour are less well documented.

HEALTH–CARE SCREENING

Health-care screening is becoming more popular in many countries and as these schemes address several aspects of health they may be more appealing than schemes designed to screen selectively for excess alcohol consumption. They present opportunities for both primary and secondary prevention. General practitioners and other health-care staff should have training in identifying individuals with current and potential alcohol problems and give appropriate advice and information about the help available.

PRIMARY HEALTH-CARE

Primary health-care provides one of the best settings for early detection of hazardous drinking and general practitioners and practice nurses should take a drinking history from all of their patients in either an opportunistic or systematic way. Many are now using quick screening tools such as the FAST version of the AUDIT questionnaire (*Appendix C*). Individuals identified as drinking in excess of recommended levels can be given advice in the form of a brief intervention and can be monitored accordingly (Chapter 6).

ACUTE HOSPITAL TRUSTS

Accident and Emergency departments provide another ideal locus for this activity, as do the acute admission units and the general wards in Acute Hospital Trusts. There is good evidence that identification in these settings coupled with focused advice can be extremely effective in changing drinking habits in a positive direction and reducing subsequent health-related harm. One of the barriers to this is the difficulty encountered in persuading busy staff of the importance of using these techniques and ensuring that the necessary training in brief intervention is available. Short screening questionnaires have been devised specifically to facilitate this process in Accident and Emergency departments, for example the PAT (*Appendix C*). In addition increasing numbers of Acute Hospital Trusts are employing specialist liaison nurses to facilitate these processes.

Antenatal services have particularly important responsibilities to monitor the drinking habits of pregnant women and to give advice about the need to abstain in early pregnancy and to minimise alcohol intake thereafter. Those drinking excessively may need specialist help to achieve these goals and thus avoid the risk of alcohol-related foetal harm.

THE WORKPLACE

Many companies operate health-screening programmes for employees which could be used to identify hazardous/harmful drinking. Some, for example, the transport industry and companies running oil rigs, take this further and require workers to submit to regular breath alcohol screening.

Many employers operate an *Alcohol in Employment* policy whose essential aim is to help preserve an effective work force by ensuring that alcohol-related problems in the workplace are recognised as early as possible, and that effective intervention is provided as expediently as possible to allow those affected to achieve positive change (*Appendix D*).

Under the terms of an alcohol policy a worker who has been identified as experiencing work-related problems because of their drinking is offered appropriate help and support to deal with these issues. If they chose not to avail themselves of this help or if they are repeatedly non-compliant, despite the support provided, then they will be dealt with *via* the normal disciplinary process. These policies should form an essential component of a company's Heath and Safety remit. They should be 'owned' by a member of the senior management team who should ensure that they are implemented.

OTHER SETTINGS

Other foci for secondary prevention of this kind include screening of clients in social work and penal settings where a history of alcohol-related problems is common. The effectiveness of interventions in these settings remains unproven.

TERTIARY PREVENTION

The process of **tertiary prevention** is more or less synonymous with treatment; it is aimed at ensuring future abstinence from alcohol or safer drinking, and preventing the development of further social, emotional, psychological and physical harm. It is essential that the range of services available is widely known and advertised and that every effort is made to ensure that they are easily accessible and equitably distributed.

LEARNING POINTS

- The prevalence of alcohol-related problems within a population reflects the level of overall alcohol consumption.

- The most effective way to reduce average *per capita* consumption is by reducing availability through taxation, pricing and legislation.

- Educational campaigns have surprisingly little effect on *per capita* consumption or on individual's drinking behaviour.

- Campaigns targeted at specific 'at risk' groups are more successful.

- Screening for hazardous drinking is cost-beneficial and cost-effective.

CHAPTER 9

THE ROLE OF HEALTH-CARE PROFESSIONALS
-personal and social responsibilities

RESPONSIBILITY TO SOCIETY

All heath-care professionals, present and future, should consider what views they wish to promote on issues such as advertising, prolonging opening hours, the availability of alcohol, and particularly cost. Alcohol has become relatively cheaper in recent years and evidence suggests that price rises would curtail further consumption. Are we justified in recommending tax rises, which might be unpopular, in an attempt to reduce the overall level of consumption and harm, and cost to the NHS, or are we content to continue picking up the tab for the ill-health which alcohol engenders without making strenuous attempts to prevent these problems at an earlier stage?

Thus, depending on their stance, health-care professionals can play an important role in promoting and supporting public health campaigns aimed at reducing the level of alcohol-related harm in the population. They can help to reinforce the benefits of measures which may, at first, appear unpopular, and point to the likely gains in reducing the level of accidents and other forms of alcohol-related harm in the local community.

Health-care professionals can also play a key role in promoting sensible drinking behaviour on a more individual basis. Of these doctors are best placed to provide information on sensible drinking behaviour and to be involved in the early detection of alcohol misuse and timely intervention. The health gains of this approach are considerable and are based on good evidence.

However, doctors are also the health-care workers most likely to experience difficulties in balancing social and professional responsibilities. For example, they may be asked by the police to provide a blood sample for measurement of alcohol levels from an individual injured in a road traffic accident. These are very difficult situations to judge but the doctor's responsibility and duty of care clearly lies with their patient. If the patient is alert and willing to cooperate then a police surgeon should be requested to obtain the necessary samples in order to ensure the correct chain of custody procedures. If the patient is unable or unwilling to provide consent then the police request will have to be refused. The Medical Defence Organisations (MDO) and the British Medical Association (BMA) can advise practitioners in these difficult circumstances. However, the GMC is clear that confidentiality should be overridden when there is the risk of serious harm to others. Future legislative change may allow samples to be obtained from individuals who are unable to provide consent but the patient's well-being should still be the doctor's prime concern.

Similar problems arise for doctors in relation to drinking and driving. In the UK the Driver Vehicle and Licensing Agency (DVLA) is legally responsible for deciding if a person is medically unfit to drive. Thus, they need to know if a licence holder has a condition that either now, or in future, may render them a danger to themselves or others when in charge of a vehicle. If a doctor knows that a patient has a drinking problem and is likely to be driving under the influence of alcohol, that patient must be told that this will impair their ability to drive and that they are legally obliged to inform the DVLA. Every reasonable effort should be made to persuade them not to drive. This may include telling their next of kin if they agree to this disclosure. If they can not be persuaded or there is evidence that they are continuing to drive contrary to advice, then the doctor should warn the patient that they intend to inform the DVLA about the drink-drive situation. Doctors who find themselves in this position should speak to a medical adviser at the DVLA, in confidence. It is essential that these conversations and decisions are fully recorded. In particular it is vital that if a doctor provides information to the DVLA they should write immediately to the patient, to confirm that a disclosure has been made. If a patient is incapable of understanding advice about drink-driving, for example because of dementia or mental health problems, then the DVLA should be informed immediately.

Similar dilemmas around the question of disclosure of confidential information may affect all health-care professionals. There are very few situations when the decision to disclose personal information without the patient's consent is deemed acceptable, even if it is considered to be in the public interest. The balance of benefit to the individual and to society has to be carefully weighed. There are circumstances in which failure to disclose information could put the patient or others at risk of death or serious harm. Equally, disclosure may assist in the prevention, detection or prosecution of a serious crime. These are difficult decisions. However, professional regulatory bodies such as the General Medical Council (GMC) and the Nursing and Midwifery Council (NMC) publish guidelines which can be consulted. In addition it would seem sensible to seek advice from colleagues, and for doctors to consult a MDO before arriving at a conclusion. In all circumstances a careful record should be kept of any decisions made so that the health-care professional is confident that their position is defensible. Where practical, patients should be told that a disclosure will or has been made and the reasons for this should be recorded.

Health-care professionals may find themselves in the difficult position of being approached for advice about drinking behaviour by family or friends either for themselves or others. It is always best to simply facilitate appropriate referral and to firmly avoid becoming personally involved in treatment.

PERSONAL RESPONSIBILITY

Health-care professionals also need to consider their own drinking behaviour and how it is perceived by those around them. Doctors, in particular, are often well known within the community and should be aware of how important it is that they behave responsibly in relation to alcohol. They should not drink while on duty even if resident or simply on call from home. Clearly they should not drink and drive. Medical students, like doctors, are expected to behave in a professional way. The GMC emphasises that medical students 'have certain privileges and responsibilities different from those of other students; because of this, different standards of behaviour are expected of them.'

Members of the health-care professions are conspicuously at risk for developing alcohol-related problems. Thus, it is important that they monitor their drinking behaviour from time to time and also encourage family, friends and colleagues to do the same. They should watch out for possible increases in the amount they drink during periods of anticipated or unexpected stress.

A health-care professional who becomes aware that their drinking is getting out of hand should seek advice and support. The services for doctors are better established than for other health-care professionals. The Medical Council on Alcohol can offer advice on where to seek help and further information on this topic is also available in 'The Misuse of Alcohol and other Drugs by Doctors' (B.M.A. 1998). The Sick Doctors Trust (0870 444 5163), the BMA's Drs for Drs (0845 920 0169) and the Doctors Support Network (08703 210642) are all easily accessed. The Practitioner Health Programme has recently been established in London. This is a free, independent and confidential service supported by a multi-professional team of doctors, specialist nurses and counsellors. It offers assessment, treatment and ongoing management of a range of mental health problems, including addictions (www.php.nhs.uk).

Greater difficulties arise, however, when a health-care professional who is drinking to excess does not seek advice and help, particularly if there is evidence that their performance is being adversely affected. The GMC provided some guidance on this point. Thus, in paragraph 41e in the Good Medical Practice (GMP) guidelines they stipulate 'You must support colleagues who have problems with performance, conduct and health' while stipulating in paragraph 43 that 'You must protect your patients from risk of harm posed by a colleague's conduct, performance or health. The safety of patients must come first at all times. If you have concerns that a colleague may not be fit to practice you must take appropriate steps without delay so that the concerns can be investigated and patients protected where necessary.'

Some individuals will feel able to approach a colleague who is drinking excessively and express their concerns;

others, too often, choose to turn a blind eye. However, if patients' safety is an issue then ensuring they are not put at risk must override other considerations. Many Medical Schools and NHS institutions have developed *Alcohol in Employment* policies which aim both to ensure early identification of alcohol misuse but also to provide support and confidential treatment for staff; arrangements are often made for staff to receive treatment outside of their own institution, in the first instance, although long-term follow-up is usually undertaken in-house. These policies provide an excellent frame work within which to work and all health-care professionals should familiarise themselves with the policies in place in their own work place (*Appendix D*). In organisation without a structured employment policy the first step in dealing with an alcohol problem, having apprised the individual concerned that this is the intention, is to alert an appropriate senior colleague, for example, a line manager, clinical head of service, or medical director. In these instances responsibility for treatment referral is usually left to the individuals' general practitioner.

In general, health-care workers who develop alcohol problems are best dealt with *via* local procedures – whether these are formalized or not. The role of regulating bodies, such as the GMC, is mainly limited to taking action on serious concerns which call into question a doctor's fitness to practise and their suitability to retain unrestricted registration. Thus, it may not be necessary to involve the GMC as a first approach. However, it is essential to involve them if local attempts at rectifying the situation are unsuccessful.

If a doctor is involved in a prosecutable offence, for example, drink-driving, they will automatically be reported to the GMC *via* the courts. Indeed the majority of doctors with drinking problems, who come to the attention of the GMC, do so because of a drink–drive offence. Thus, the GMC becomes involved not only because of the criminal conviction but also because of the underlying health issues. However, the criminal conviction takes precedence. If the doctor's fitness to practice is considered to be impaired then evidence of ill-health may be taken into consideration in determining the conditions imposed. Individuals with drinking problems who are seen by the GMC with or without a criminal conviction are assessed, referred for treatment and appropriate monitoring and if they comply, are then supported to return to an active working life.

Data on outcomes are not easily accessed. However, the Doctor's and Dentist's group have published encouraging data on the long term follow-up of 100 doctors who joined the group between 1980 and 1988 (Figure 9.1). Overall, 73% recovered and are either currently abstinent or were abstinent at the time of their death. In 2001, up-to-date information was available on 80 of the original cohort; a total of 24 had died of an alcohol-related illness but of the 56 survivors 29 were still employed and 27 had retired from active practice. However, these data very much reflect the outcome in individuals who acknowledge that they have a problem and are prepared to do something about it.

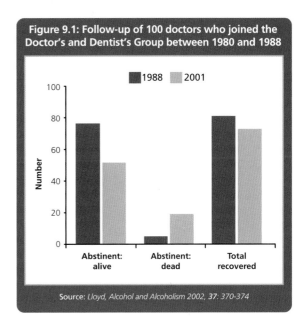

Figure 9.1: Follow-up of 100 doctors who joined the Doctor's and Dentist's Group between 1980 and 1988

Source: Lloyd, Alcohol and Alcoholism 2002, *37*: 370-374

The GMC figures are, in contrast, much less sanguine reflecting perhaps the seriousness of the problems of the individuals referred to them and also because they reflect outcomes in both those who comply with advice and those who do not. Of those who agree to certain undertakings and escape a fitness to practice hearing one-third will regain full registration within a ten year period. However, of those who appear at a GMC fitness to practice hearing, either because they do not agree/fail to comply with undertakings, or the circumstances are sufficiently serious that undertakings are not appropriate, only one in ten regain unrestricted registration after ten years and a third will no longer be registered.

LEARNING POINTS

- Health–care professionals have responsibilities, as informed members of the public, to promulgate sensible views on alcohol consumption and alcohol policy and to lead by example.

- Patient confidentiality is of paramount importance but when a patient's drinking is putting others at risk a breach of that confidentiality can be justified, if other measures of persuasion have failed.

- Health-care workers are at increased risk of developing alcohol-related problems and should monitor their own alcohol consumption and encourage others to do likewise.

- Significant difficulties arise if a colleague develops a drinking problem and will not address it. Local solutions should be sought if at all possible.

- Recalcitrant drinkers and those posing a significant risk to patients should be referred to their professional body.

- The outcome for health-care workers with an alcohol problem who accept their problem and comply with advice is probably as good, if not better, than for the general public.

APPENDICES

APPENDIX A

THE ALCOHOL CONTENT OF BEVERAGES

Beverage Type	Alcohol by Volume (%)	Measure	Alcohol Content (units)
BEERS/LAGERS/STOUTS:			
Barbican	0.02	440 ml	0
Kaliber	0.05	Pint	0.03
Swan Light	0.5	Pint	0.3
Tennents LA	1.2	440 ml	0.5
Mild/light beers (various brands)	3.1	Pint	1.8
Best bitter (various brands)	3.5	Pint	2.0
Carlsberg Pils	3.6	440 ml	1.6
Skol	3.6	500 ml	1.8
Carling Black Label	4.0	440 ml	1.8
		Pint	2.3
Guinness draft stout	4.1	440 ml	1.8
		Pint	2.3
Desperados lager (with blackcurrant)	5.9	330 ml	1.9
Grolsch	5.0	440 ml	2.2
Stella Artois	5.2	330 ml	1.7
		440 ml	2.3
		Pint	3.0
Lowenbrau Pils	6.0	440 ml	2.6
Fullers 1845	6.3	500 ml	3.2
Hofmeister Special	9.0	440 ml	4.0
Kestral Super	9.5	440 ml	4.2
'DESIGNER DRINKS':			
Hoopers Hooch alcoholic lemon	4.7	330 ml	1.6
Hoopers alcoholic apple	5.0	330 ml	1.7
Shotts tangerine scream	5.3	330 ml	1.7
Barcardi breezers	5.4	200 ml	1.1
		275 ml	1.5
Archers	5.5	275 ml	1.5
Smirnoff ice	5.5	275 ml	1.5
		700 ml	3.9
WKD original blue	5.5	330 ml	1.8
		700 ml	3.9
MD20/20	13.0	187 ml	2.4

Beverage Type	Alcohol by Volume (%)	Measure	Alcohol Content (units)
CIDERS/PERRIES:			
Strongbow LA	0.9	330 ml	0.3
Woodpecker	4.0	440 ml	1.8
		1000 ml	4.0
Strongbow	4.5	440 ml	2.0
		1000 ml	4.5
Max black (with blackcurrent)	5.0	275 ml	1.4
Babycham	6.0	200 ml	1.2
Woodpecker red	7.4	275 ml	2.0
Diamond White	7.5	275 ml	2.1
		440 ml	3.3
Merrydown Vintage	8.2	330 ml	2.7
Strong White Cider	8.4	1000 ml	8.4
WINES/FORTIFIED WINES:			
Eisberg German white	0.05	750 ml	0.04
Lambrusco white	5.0	750 ml	3.8
Blue Nun white	10.0	750 ml	7.5
Mateus Rosè	11.0	750 ml	8.3
Le Piat D'Or red	11.0	750 ml	8.3
Bulls Blood red	12.0	750 ml	9.0
Moët et Chandon Brut	12.0	750 ml	9.0
Cinzano bianco	14.7	750 ml	11.0
Buckfast tonic wine	15.0	750 ml	11.0
Crofts original sherry	17.5	750 ml	13.1
Cockburn's Port	20.0	750 ml	15.0
SPIRITS:			
Gordon's dry gin	37.5	700 ml	26.3
Smirnoff vodka	37.5	700 ml	26.3
Bacardi white rum	37.5	700 ml	26.3
		1000 ml	37.5
Bells whisky	40.0	700 ml	28.0
Martell cognac brandy	40.0	700 ml	28.0
Captain Morgan's dark rum	40.0	700 ml	28.0
		1000 ml	40.0
LIQUEURS:			
Advocaat	15.0	700 ml	10.5
Bailey's Irish cream	17.0	350 ml	6.0
Apricot brandy	24.0	700 ml	16.8
Creme de Menthe	24.0	700 ml	16.8
Malibu	24.0	700 ml	16.8
Pernod	40.0	700 ml	28.0
Cointreau	40.0	700 ml	28.0
Drambuie	40.0	700 ml	28.0

APPENDIX B

ALCOHOL AND THE LAW

Alcohol is a legal drug but it affects mood and behaviour particularly when taken in excess. Laws have, therefore, been developed to marshal these effects and behaviours. The following is not an exhaustive discussion of this topic but it does touch on the most common and most concerning issues.

DRUNK AND DISORDERLY

The majority of incidents of 'Being drunk and disorderly in a public place' are categorised as public nuisance offences. The number of people charged with this offence has fallen quite dramatically in the UK over the last fifty years despite a significant increase in alcohol consumption over the same period. However, this reduction in prosecutions is not a reflection of a reduction in the number of offences being committed but rather a reflection of the falling priority of this offence as well as the sheer practicalities of policing large numbers of drunken people.[1]

However, there is always the potential that these offences might escalate into more serious offences particularly involving violence. The British Crime Survey (2007/08),[2] reported that in nearly 1 million violent attacks in 2007/08 the aggressors were believed to be drunk. This equates to 45% of all violent incidents that occurred: moreover, in violent incidents in which the aggressor was not previously known to the victim this figure rose to 58%. In cases of domestic violence, 37% involved alcohol.

DRINK AND DRIVING

It is illegal to drive, in the UK, with a breath alcohol in excess of 35 µg/100 ml or a blood alcohol in excess of 80 ml/100 ml (22 mMol/l). In contrast the legal limit for driving in most other European countries is lower, usually a blood alcohol level in excess of 50 mg/100 ml (13.5 mMol/L).

Any person who is driving, attempting to drive, or in charge of a motor vehicle on the road, or in a public place, for example, a pub car park or a garage forecourt, may be required by the police to provide a breath test to determine whether they are over the prescribed limit of alcohol for driving. The Police can, however, only insist on a breath test if they have reasonable cause to suspect that excess alcohol has been consumed, that a traffic offence has been committed or is being committed or that there has been involvement in a traffic–related accident.

If the road-side breath test is positive or if a breath sample can not be provided or the request is refused then the person involved is arrested and taken to the police station where they will be required to provide two breath specimens using an evidential machine. If the two readings differ then the police must rely on the lower reading, which, if over the prescribed limit, will result in a charge. Individuals do not have the right, under these circumstances, to insist on an alternative or confirmatory blood or urine test. Failure to produce or supply a breath test at the station is an offence, unless there is a mitigating circumstance such as asthma, which prevents adequate breath sampling. Being too drunk or unfit to supply the necessary specimen is not a reasonable excuse. Under these circumstances the individual has a right to request a blood or urine sample, which must be taken by a police surgeon and the chain of custody assured. Detainees can request a second sample for their own retention for independent analysis.

If the lower of the two breath tests is ≤ 39 µg/100ml then the detainee will be released without charge. If the lower value is between 40 and 50 µg/100 ml then the police must offer the detainee a chance to provide a confirmatory blood or urine sample under the same conditions as mentioned above. Detainees whose lower breath test reading exceeds 50 µg/100 ml are charged with a drink-drive offence the nature of which will determine the outcome viz:

[1] Institute of Alcohol Studies Fact Sheet: Alcohol-related Crime and Disorder, 2007
[2] www.homeoffice.gov.uk/rds/pdfs08/hosb0708

Failure to provide a roadside breath test: results in a fine of up to £1000 with four penalty points on the licence. Disqualification is at the discretion of the court but is almost invariable.

Driving/attempting to drive with excess alcohol: results in a fine of up to £5000 **and/or** up to 6 months imprisonment plus mandatory disqualification for at least 12 months for a first offence, or mandatory disqualification for at least three years for a second offence within 10 years.

Being in charge of a motor vehicle with excess alcohol: results in a fine of up to £2500 **and/or** up to 3 months imprisonment, with 10 penalty points on the licence. Disqualification is again at the court's discretion.

After driving/attempting to drive and then refusing to provide samples for analysis: results in a fine up to £5000 **and/or** 6 months imprisonment with mandatory disqualification for at least 12 months for a first offence, and at least 3 years for a second offence.

After being in charge refusing to provide samples for analysis: results in a fine of £2500 **and/or** 3 months imprisonment, with 10 points on the licence. Disqualification is again at the court's discretion.

It is possible for courts to consider reinstating a licence originally removed for more than 2 years if, after two years, the court is satisfied that no further road traffic offences have been committed and/or there are extenuating circumstances to consider earlier reinstatement such as a new job which requires a current driving licence. Similarly offenders may attend a recognised education programme, at their own expense, after disqualification which may result in earlier reinstatement.[3]

Significant changes to this system are expected which have not yet been released into the public domain but which might include the use of evidential breathalysers at the road side and abolition of the right to request an alternative or confirmatory blood or urine test. In addition some form of random breath testing may be introduced.

Drink-Driving Statistics in the UK

- On average 3000 people are killed or seriously injured each year in drink-drive collisions.

- Nearly one in six of all deaths on the road involve drivers over the legal limit.

- Drinking and driving occurs across a wide range of age groups but particularly among young men.

- Provisional figures for 2004, for drivers over the legal limit, show 590 people killed, 2350 seriously injured and 14 050 slightly injured.

- More than half a million breath tests are carried out each year, of which 100 000 are positive.

The Road Traffic Act 1991 states that: *'A person who causes the death of another person by driving a mechanically propelled vehicle dangerously on a road or other public place is guilty of an offence.'* The maximum penalty for this offence was increased to 10 years by the Criminal Justice Act 1993, and was further increased to 14 years in 2003. Disqualification for a minimum period of two years is obligatory and the licence is endorsed with 3 to 11 penalty points.

Alcohol, your Child and the Law

Laws exist in the UK which govern alcohol consumption by children.[4]

- **Under five-year-olds**
  It is illegal to give alcohol to a child under five except under medical supervision in an emergency.

---

[3] www.lawontheweb.co.uk/crimedrinkdriving.htm 2009
[4] www.direct.gov.uk

- **Under 16-year-olds**
  Children under 16 can go anywhere in a pub, as long as they are supervised by an adult, but they are not allowed to consume alcohol. However, some premises may be subject to licensing conditions which prevent them from allowing entry to under 16-year-olds, for example, those that have experienced problems with underage drinking.

- **16 or 17-year-olds**
  Young people aged 16 or 17 can drink beer, wine or cider with a meal if it is bought for them by an adult and they are accompanied by an adult while drinking. It is illegal for them to drink spirits in pubs even with a meal.

  In Scotland, 16 and 17-year-olds can buy beer, wine or cider as long as it is served with a meal and consumed in an area used solely for dining.

- **Under 18-year-olds**
  It is against the law for anyone under the age of 18 to buy alcohol in a pub, off-licence, supermarket, or other outlet, or for anyone to buy alcohol for someone under 18 to consume in a pub or a public place. Similarly it is illegal for members of staff in on-and off-licence premises to knowingly sell alcohol to anyone under the age of 18. Some towns and cities have local by-laws banning the consumption of alcohol in public by individuals of all ages.

The maximum penalty for retailers supplying products to persons under the age of 18 are:
- A £5000 fine plus a possible review of their licence plus an £80 fixed penalty notice for the vendor;
- A maximum £10 000 fine if persistently found to be selling to children.

The police have the power, under the confiscation of Alcohol (Young Persons) Act 1997, to confiscate alcohol from under 18-year-olds drinking in public places who are creating a disorder or where the officer holds a reasonable belief that the child will consume the alcohol.

Alcohol and Child Protection

According to the Government's alcohol strategy for England,[5] between 780 000 and 1.3 million children are affected by parental alcohol problems.

Parental substance use was considered to be a concern by social workers in 52% of 50 families with 95 children living in an inner London area; alcohol was a concern in 24% and heroin in 16%.[6] There was a strong association between parental substance misuse and child neglect with double the likelihood that these families will be subjected to care proceedings.[7] Tellingly few if any of these families were in contact with substance abuse professionals.

For a full discussion of this topic refer to: www.alcoholandfamilies.org.uk

Alcohol and the Mental Health Act

It is not possible to detain patients under the Mental Health Act (1983) simply because they are alcohol dependent. If there is a co-existing mental health disorder that puts the individual, or those around them at risk, then the Act can be applied.

---

[5] Alcohol Harm Reduction Strategy for England, Cabinet Office, 2004
[6] Forrester, Child Abuse Review 9.4:235-246, 2000
[7] Forrester and Harwin, Parents who Misuse Drugs and Alcohol: Effective Interventions in Social Work and Child Protection, 2009

APPENDIX C

ALCOHOL SCREENING QUESTIONNAIRES

THE MICHIGAN ALCOHOL SCREENING TEST (MAST)

	Please answer YES or NO to the following questions:	YES	NO
1	Do you feel you are a normal drinker? ('normal' - drink as much or less than most other people)		
2	Have you ever awakened the morning after some drinking the night before and found that you could not remember a part of the evening?		
3	Does any near relative or close friend ever worry or complain about your drinking?		
4	Can you stop drinking without difficulty after one or two drinks?		
5	Do you ever feel guilty about your drinking?		
6	Have you ever attended a meeting of Alcoholics Anonymous (AA)?		
7	Have you ever gotten into physical fights when drinking?		
8	Has drinking ever created problems between you and a near relative or close friend?		
9	Has any family member or close friend gone to anyone for help about your drinking?		
10	Have you ever lost friends because of your drinking?		
11	Have you ever gotten into trouble at work because of drinking?		
12	Have you ever lost a job because of drinking?		
13	Have you ever neglected your obligations, your family, or your work for two or more days in a row because you were drinking?		
14	Do you drink before noon fairly often?		
15	Have you ever been told you have liver trouble such as cirrhosis?		
16	After heavy drinking have you ever had delirium tremens (DTs), severe shaking, visual or auditory (hearing) hallucinations?		
17	Have you ever gone to anyone for help about your drinking?		
18	Have you ever been hospitalized because of drinking?		
19	Has your drinking ever resulted in your being hospitalized in a psychiatric ward?		
20	Have you ever gone to any doctor, social worker, clergyman or mental health clinic for help with any emotional problem in which drinking was part of the problem?		
21	Have you been arrested more than once for driving under the influence of alcohol?		
22	Have you ever been arrested, even for a few hours, because of other behaviour while drinking?		

SCORING

Score 1 point for each 'yes' answer — except for questions 1 and 4, where

1 point is allocated for each 'no' answer — and then total the responses.

0 - 2 No apparent problem; 3 - 5 Early or middle problem drinker ≥ 6 Problem drinker

TOTAL points scored

THE SHORT MAST–GERIATRIC VERSION (SMAST-G)

	Please answer YES or NO to the following questions:	YES	NO
1	When talking with others, do you ever underestimate how much you drink?		
2	After a few drinks, have you sometimes not eaten or been able to skip a meal because you didn't feel hungry?		
3	Does having a few drinks help decrease your shakiness or tremors?		
4	Does alcohol sometimes make it hard for you to remember parts of the day or night?		
5	Do you usually take a drink to relax or calm your nerves?		
6	Do you drink to take your mind off your problems?		
7	Have you ever increased your drinking after experiencing a loss in your life?		
8	Has a doctor or nurse ever said they were worried or concerned about your drinking?		
9	Have you ever made rules to manage your drinking?		
10	When you feel lonely, does having a drink help?		

SCORING

Score 1 point to each 'yes' answer and total the responses.

Scores ≥ 2 are indicative of an alcohol problem

TOTAL points scored

THE ALCOHOL USE DISORDERS IDENTIFICATION TEST (AUDIT)

Circle the number that comes closest to the patient's answer

1 How often do you have a drink containing alcohol?*

(0) NEVER   (1) LESS THAN MONTHLY   (2) TWO TO FOUR TIMES A MONTH   (3) TWO TO THREE TIMES A WEEK   (4) FOUR OR MORE TIMES A WEEK

2 How many drinks containing alcohol do you have on a typical day when you are drinking? (Code number of standard drinks)

(0) 1 OR 2   (1) 3 OR 4   (2) 5 OR 6   (3) 7 OR 8   (4) 10 OR MORE

3 How often do you have six or more drinks on one occasion?

(0) NEVER   (1) LESS THAN MONTHLY   (2) MONTHLY   (3) WEEKLY   (4) DAILY OR ALMOST DAILY

4 How often during the last year have you found that you were not able to stop drinking once you had started?

(0) NEVER   (1) LESS THAN MONTHLY   (2) MONTHLY   (3) WEEKLY   (4) DAILY OR ALMOST DAILY

5 How often during the last year have you failed to do what was normally expected from you because of drinking?

(0) NEVER   (1) LESS THAN MONTHLY   (2) MONTHLY   (3) WEEKLY   (4) DAILY OR ALMOST DAILY

6 How often during the last year have you needed a first drink in the morning to get yourself going after a heavy drinking session?

(0) NEVER   (1) LESS THAN MONTHLY   (2) MONTHLY   (3) WEEKLY   (4) DAILY OR ALMOST DAILY

7 How often during the last year have you had a feeling of guilt or remorse after drinking?

(0) NEVER   (1) LESS THAN MONTHLY   (2) MONTHLY   (3) WEEKLY   (4) DAILY OR ALMOST DAILY

8 How often during the last year have you been unable to remember what happened the night before because you had been drinking?

(0) NEVER   (1) LESS THAN MONTHLY   (2) MONTHLY   (3) WEEKLY   (4) DAILY OR ALMOST DAILY

9 Have you or someone else been injured as a result of your drinking?

(0) NO   (1) YES, BUT NOT IN THE LAST YEAR   (2) YES, DURING THE LAST YEAR

10 Has a relative or friend or a doctor or other health worker been concerned about your drinking or suggested you cut down?

(0) NO   (1) YES, BUT NOT IN THE LAST YEAR   (2) YES, DURING THE LAST YEAR

SCORING

A score of ≥ 8 gives the highest sensitivity

* In determining the response categories it has been assumed that one 'drink' contains 10 g alcohol. In countries where the alcohol content of a standard drink differs by more than 25% from 10 g, the response category should be modified accordingly.

THE FAST ALCOHOL SCREENING TEST (FAST)

For the following questions please circle the answer which best applies

1 drink = ½ pint of beer or 1 glass of wine or 1 single spirits

1   MEN: How often do you have EIGHT or more drinks on one occasion?
     WOMEN: How often do you have SIX or more drinks on one occasion?

| NEVER | LESS THAN MONTHLY | MONTHLY | WEEKLY | DAILY OR ALMOST DAILY |

2   How often during the last year have you been unable to remember what happened the night before because you had been drinking?

| NEVER | LESS THAN MONTHLY | MONTHLY | WEEKLY | DAILY OR ALMOST DAILY |

3   How often during the last year have you failed to do what was normally expected of you because of drinking

| NEVER | LESS THAN MONTHLY | MONTHLY | WEEKLY | DAILY OR ALMOST DAILY |

4   In the last year has a relative or friend, or a doctor or other health worker been concerned about your drinking or suggested you cut down?

| NO | YES, ON ONE OCCASION | YES, ON MORE THAN ONE OCCASION |

SCORING

Score questions 1-3: 0, 1, 2, 3, 4. Score question 4: 0, 2, 4.

A score ≥3 indicates probable hazardous drinking

THE PADDINGTON ALCOHOL TEST (PAT)

After dealing with the patient's reasons for attendance to A&E, ask the following questions:

1. Quite a number of people have times when they drink more than usual; what is the most you will drink in any one day?

   (Note: 1 unit = 8 g alcohol. Pub measures are given in brackets; homes measures of 'singles,' for example, are often x 3):

Beer/lager/cider	☐ Pints (2)	☐ Cans (1.5)	
Strong beer/lager/cider	☐ Pints (5)	☐ Cans (4)	
Wine	☐ Glasses (1.5)	☐ Bottles (9)	
Fortified wine (sherry, martini)	☐ Glasses (1)	☐ Bottles (12)	
Spirits (gin, whisky, vodka)	☐ Singles (1)	☐ Bottles (30)	Total units/day ☐

2. If you sometime drink more than 8 units/day (for men), or 6 units/day (for women), is this at least once a week?

   YES = PAT +ve
   NO = GO TO Question 3

3. Do you feel your current A&E attendance is related to alcohol?

   YES = PAT +ve
   NO = PAT −ve

   Patients who are PAT +ve should be offered specific alcohol advice and managed according to a local protocol

THE CAGE AND T-ACE QUESTIONNAIRES

CAGE	T-ACE
C - Have you ever felt you should **cut down** on your drinking?	**T** - **Tolerance:** How many drinks does it take to make you feel high?
A - Have people **annoyed** you by criticizing your drinking?	**A** - Have people **annoyed** you by criticizing your drinking?
G - Have you ever felt bad or **guilty** about your drinking?	**C** - Have you ever felt you should **cut down** on your drinking?
E - **Eye opener:** Have you ever had a drink first thing in the morning to steady your nerves or to get rid of a hangover?	**E** - **Eye opener:** Have you ever had a drink first thing in the morning to steady your nerves or to get rid of a hangover?
Two positive responses indicate a positive test and the need for further assessment.	The T-ACE is based on the CAGE and is particularly useful for prenatal/antenatal screening An affirmative answer of 'more than two drinks' to the first question: Score = 2 Affirmative answers to the remaining three questions: Score = 1 each An overall score of 2 or more is considered positive.

APPENDIX D

WORKPLACE ALCOHOL POLICIES

The costs associated with alcohol problems at work and the impact of current legislation suggests that alcohol policies are becoming an essential part of good employment practice. The Government's 'Health, Work and Well-Being' initiative, launched in 2005, encourages and supports employers in their initiatives to improve the health and well-being of their employees.

Key Principles of an Alcohol Policy

An alcohol policy does not have to be a long and complicated document. However, it is helpful to clarify certain points with regard to its implementation.

CLEAR STATEMENT OF INTENT

A policy should be a written statement of intent outlining how the organization will deal with the issue of alcohol/problem drinking at work.

COMMITMENT TO JOINT NEGOTIATION

For a policy to work in practice it should be based on joint negotiation and/or consultation between management, trade unions and/or employee representatives.

CLEARLY STATED POLICY OBJECTIVES

Policy objectives generally fall into:

- Prevention of alcohol problems at work;

- Commitment to ensuring the health, safety and well-being of employees;

- Ensuring that the policy makes it clear whether or not employees are allowed to consume alcohol at work, drink during working hours or drink before attending work;

- Making sure that the policy includes information about the level of support, including counselling or professional help, that an employee will receive if an alcohol problem is recognised;

- Procedures for defining the role and responsibilities of management when dealing with alcohol problems at work;

- Providing employees with information on the effects of alcohol and sources of support.

IT IS APPLICABLE TO ALL EMPLOYEES?

A policy should be applicable to all employees, regardless of status.

CONFIDENTIALITY

The maintenance of strict confidentiality is fundamental to an alcohol policy.

Alcohol Policies in the NHS

The Department of Health report 'High Quality Care for All: Our Journey so Far,' published in 2009, makes it clear that the health and well-being of NHS staff is of paramount importance.

Sample Statement of Intent for an NHS Trust

Alcohol, even in small amounts, can compromise motor skills, impede judgement and negatively affects performance. Therefore, *the NHS Trust* believes that the influence of alcohol at any time during the working day or night is not in line with the professional standards expected of all health-care professionals employed by *the Trust*.

Rule:

Throughout the working day, each person must be fully fit for work at the best of their ability in order to carry out their duties as an employee of *the Trust*. There should be no impairment at all to his or her conduct or performance that is linked to the consumption of alcohol.

Rule:

There must be no consumption of alcohol on *Trust* premises at any time during the working day, nor should alcohol be consumed off premises during the working day. All health-care employees should approach the matter of drinking alcohol with the maximum of responsibility and self-control. If the highest standards of responsibility are not maintained in this respect, the management will take sanctions in order to protect the position of other *Trust* employees and crucially of patients.

Should any of the above rules be breached, disciplinary action will be taken.

Health-care employees are strongly advised by *the Trust* not to consume alcohol off the premises at any time during break times or between shifts during the working day.

APPENDIX E

SUGGESTED READING

Anderson P, Chisholm D, Fuhr DC. Effectiveness and cost-effectiveness of policies and programmes to reduce the harm caused by alcohol. *Lancet* 2009; **373**: 2234-2246.

BMA Board of Science. Alcohol misuse; tackling the UK epidemic. London: BMA, 2008.

Casswell S, Thamarangsi T. Reducing harm from alcohol: call to action. *Lancet* 2009; **373**: 2247-2257.

Health Technology Board for Scotland. *Prevention of Relapse in Alcohol Dependence*. Edinburgh: NHS Scotland, 2002.

Henderson J, Kesmodel U, Gray R. Systematic review of the foetal effects of prenatal binge drinking. *Journal of Epidemiology and Community Health* 2007; **61**:1069-1073.

Jarvis TJ, Tebbutt, Mattick RP, Shand F. *Treatment Approaches for Alcohol and Drug Dependence*. Chichester: John Wiley and Sons Ltd, 2005.

Marjot D, *The Disease of Alcohol*. London: Southern Universities Press, 2009.

Mayfield RD, Harris RA, Schuckit MA. Genetic factors influencing alcohol dependence. *British Journal of Pharmacology* 2008; **154**: 275-287.

Miller WR, Rollnick S. *Motivational Interviewing*. London: Guilford Press, 2002.

Plant M, Plant M. *Binge Britain*. Oxford: Oxford University Press, 2006.

Raistrick D, Heather N, Godfrey C. *Review of the Effectiveness for Treatment of Alcohol Problems*. London: National Treatment Agency for Substance Misuse, 2006.

Raistrick D, Hodgson R, Ritson B. *Tackling Alcohol Together*. London: Free Association Books, 1999.

Rehm J, Mathers C, Popova S, Thavorncharoensap M, Teerawattananon Y, Patra J. Global burden of disease and injury and economic cost attributable to alcohol use and alcohol-use disorders. *Lancet* 2009; **373**: 2223-2233.

Royal College of Physicians. *Alcohol-can the NHS afford it?* Recommendations for a coherent alcohol strategy for hospitals. London: Royal College of Physicians, 2002.

Statistics on Alcohol: England 2009. The NHS Information Centre for Health and Social Care. Available on www.ic.nhs.uk

Scottish Executive. *Plan of Action on Alcohol Problems*. Edinburgh: Scottish Executive Health Department, 2002.

Scottish Intercollegiate Network Guidelines. *The Management of Harmful Drinking and Alcohol Dependence in Primary Care*. Scotland: SIGA, 2003.

Tober G, Raistrick D. *Motivational Dialogue*. London: Routledge, 2007.

Wagenaar AC, Salois MJ, Komro KA. Effects of beverage alcohol price and tax levels on drinking: a meta-analysis of 1003 estimates from 112 studies. *Addiction* 2009; **104**: 179-190.

White IR, Altmann DR, Nanchahal K. Alcohol consumption and mortality; modelling risks for men and women at different ages. *British Medical Journal* 2002; **325**:191-198.

White IR, Altmann DR, Nanchahal K. Mortality in England and Wales attributable to any drinking, drinking above sensible limits and drinking above lowest-risk level. *Addiction* 2004; **99**:749-756.

APPENDIX F

PROJECTS AND EXERCISES

CHAPTER 1: ALCOHOL, ITS METABOLISM AND CONSUMPTION

- Sample a group of colleagues and identify how much they know about the unit system of measuring alcohol content and the strengths of different alcoholic beverages.

- What are the advantages and disadvantages of labelling alcoholic drinks in terms of units or in terms of strengths? Is this knowledge helpful for health promotion?

- Describe the metabolic pathway for alcohol and the factors that influence it.

- Detail the effects of alcohol as its blood concentration increases from zero to 400 mg/100 ml (86.8 mMol/l) in (i) a non-habitual drinker and (ii) an habitual drinker.

- Discuss the clinical use of guidelines for sensible drinking.

CHAPTER 2: PREDISPOSITION TO PROBLEM DRINKING AND ALCOHOL-RELATED HARM

- What are the factors that determine an individual's propensity to develop harmful drinking and alcohol dependence? What are the implications of these findings for health promotion and advice to patients and their relatives?

- What are the factors which determine an individual's susceptibility to develop alcohol-related physical harm?

CHAPTER 3: ALCOHOL-RELATED PHYSICAL HARM

- What constitute the most important physical consequence of excess alcohol consumption?

- Detail the acute and chronic effects of alcohol misuse on physical well-being.

- What is the most important management goal in patients with alcohol-related physical harm? How may it be facilitated?

- What are the effects of alcohol, when drunk to excess, in pregnant women? How may they be avoided?

CHAPTER 4: ALCOHOL-RELATED SOCIAL AND PSYCHOLOGICAL HARM

- A large number of the social problems related to drinking arise from intoxication and its consequences. Think about these consequences from a health point of view; find out about the prevalence of alcohol-related problems in the Accident and Emergency department and the way in which they are patterned throughout the week. Consider the cost implications for the work of the Health Service in this area, e.g. accidents, domestic violence, fights, head injury, acute gastritis and alcohol-related self-harm. Review these figures for some of the wards and departments you know well.

CHAPTER 5: THE DETECTION AND ASSESSMENT OF ALCOHOL MISUSE

- What features would make you suspect that an individual was misusing alcohol?

- If you were asked to provide information on the drinking behaviour of a group of patients how would you tackle this:

  a) if allowed to interview the patients
  b) if not allowed to have any contact with the patients

- Keep a diary of your own drinking and consider the situations in which you are most likely to drink alcohol. Also, keep a diary of your other habits such as drinking coffee. Think how you would change these habits or better still, experiment with change and get to understand the difficulties that may arise.

- What are the relative merits of screening questionnaires and how best might they be employed?

CHAPTER 6: THE MANAGEMENT OF ALCOHOL MISUSE

- Alcohol-related problems are very diverse and have a spectrum of severity. How would you organize a service to ensure that the treatment was appropriately matched to the needs of the individual patient? Where would points of contact for early intervention be best placed to achieve the maximum impact?

- What role is there for pharmacotherapy in the management of individuals dependent on alcohol?

- What additional problems do vulnerable groups, for example ethnic minorities, adolescents, the elderly and the prison population pose for existing services?

CHAPTER 7:THE MANAGEMENT OF SPECIFIC ALCOHOL-RELATED PROBLEMS

- How best might an aggressive intoxicated individual be managed, and by whom?

- What are the advantages and disadvantages of treating alcohol withdrawal in the community?

- What considerations must be taken into account when prescribing drugs for individuals who misuse alcohol? What additional precautions should be taken in individuals with alcohol-related liver disease?

CHAPTER 8: THE PREVENTION OF ALCOHOL-RELATED HARM

- What is the most effective way to reduce average *per capita* consumption and how might this be achieved?

- Prevention is better than cure, and yet many services are devoted to treating the end-stages of excessive drinking and alcohol dependence. Why is this?

- Devise a way of ensuring that all doctors enquire about and remind their patients about sensible drinking. What barriers might prevent this happening on a regular basis and how might this be overcome?

- Consider the implications of what is known about the influence of the availability of alcohol on individual consumption. Do doctors have a role to play in influencing this? Consider examples of enhanced availability in your local university, medical school and community and how you might seek to influence these.

CHAPTER 9: THE ROLE OF HEALTH-CARE PROFESSIONALS

- Consider the responsibility that health-care professionals have towards the use of alcohol in society and the way it is presented to the consumer. Do these professionals have an important part to play as 'role models'?

- Patient confidentiality is of paramount importance. Under what circumstances could a breach of that confidentiality be justified?

- If you became aware that a fellow student or a professional colleague was drinking too much how would you handle it? Where could you obtain help and advice?

APPENDIX G

USEFUL CONTACTS

 A Agencies offering information, advice, guidance and access for support and treatment for those affected by alcohol (and other drug) misuse.

THE MEDICAL COUNCIL ON ALCOHOL
5 St Andrews Place,
Regent's Park,
London, NW1 4LB

Telephone: 0207 487 4445
E-mail: mca@medicouncil.demon.co.uk
Website: www.medicouncilalcol.demon.co.uk

THE SICK DOCTORS TRUST
The Belfry,
Blackstone,
Henfield,
West Sussex, BN5 9TE

Telephone: 0870 444 5163 (24 hours)
E-mail: help@sick-doctors-trust.co.uk
Website: www.sick-doctors-trust.co.uk

A 24-hour advice and intervention service for doctors.

THE BRITISH DOCTORS AND DENTIST GROUP   Telephone: 0207 487 4445 (*via* the MCA)

A support group of recovering medical and dental alcohol and drug misusers.
Students also welcomed.

THE ASSOCIATION OF ANAESTHETISTS
21 Portland Place,
London, W1B 1PY

Telephone: 0207 631 1650 (*via* Welfare Committee)
E-mail: wellbeing@aagbi.org
Website: www.aagbi.org/memberswellbeing.htm

Operates a scheme for anaesthetists including those in training.

PRACTITIONERS HEALTH PROGRAMME
Riverside Medical Centre,
Hobart House,
St George Wharf,
Wandsworth Road,
Vauxhall,
London, SW8 2JB

Telephone: 0203 049 4505
E-mail: php.help@nhs.net
Website: www.php.nhs.uk

Offers a free, confidential service for doctors and dentists in London.

BMA COUNSELLING SERVICE
Doctors for doctors helpline

Telephone: 0845 920 0169
Website: www.bma.org.uk/doctorsfordoctors

B Agencies offering information and literature on alcohol, alcohol dependence and drinking problems.

THE MEDICAL COUNCIL ON ALCOHOL
5 St Andrews Place,
Regent's Park,
London, NW1 4LB

Telephone: 0207 487 4445
E-mail: mca@medicouncil.demon.co.uk
Website: www.medicouncilalcol.demon.co.uk

HEALTH DEVELOPMENT AGENCY
7th Floor Holborn Gate,
330 High Holborn,
London, WC1B 7BA

Telephone: 0207 487 4479
Fax: 0207 935 4479
E-mail: communications@had-online.org.uk
Website: www.had-online.org.uk

ALCOHOL CONCERN
64 Leman Street,
London, E1 8EU

Telephone: 0207 264 0510
E-mail: contact@alcoholconcern.org.uk
Website: www.alcoholconcern.org.uk

ALCOHOL FOCUS SCOTLAND
2nd Floor, 166 Buchanan Street,
Glasgow, G1 2NH

Telephone: 0141 572 6700
E-mail: enquiries@alcohol-focus-scotland.org.uk
Website: www.alcohol-focus-scotland.org.uk

ALCOHOLICS ANONYMOUS
General Service Office,
PO Box 1, 10 Toft Green,
York, YO1 7ND

Telephone: 01904 644 026 (Administration)
0207 352 3001 (Helpline 10am-10pm)
Website: www.alcoholics-anonymous.org.uk/
www.aa-gb.org.uk

AL-ANON FAMILY GROUPS
61 Great Dover Street,
London, SE1 6YF

Telephone: 0207 403 0888 (Helpline 10am-10pm)
Fax: 0207 378 9910
E-mail: enquiries@al-anonuk.org.uk
Website: www.al-anonuk.org.uk

THE INSTITUTE OF ALCOHOL STUDIES
Alliance House,
12 Caxton Street,
London, SW1H 0QS

Telephone: 0207 222 4001/5880
Fax: 0207 799 2510
E-mail: info@ias.org.uk
Web site: www.ias.org.uk

Elmgren House,
1 The Quay, St Ives,
Cambridgeshire, PE27 5AR

Telephone: 01480 466766
Fax: 01480 497583

ALCOHOL EDUCATION RESEARCH COUNCIL
EH 1.4 - Eliot House,
10-12 Allington Street,
London, SW1E 5EH

Telephone: 0207 808 7150
Fax: 0207 808 7151
E-mail: andrea.tilouche@aerc.org.uk
Website: www.aerc.org.uk

APPENDIX H

MCA PUBLICATIONS AND ACTIVITIES

PUBLICATIONS:

- Journal: *Alcohol and Alcoholism*
  The International Journal of the Medical Council on Alcohol and the European Society for Biomedical Research on Alcoholism (ESBRA).
  Published bimonthly: www.oxfordjournals.org/our_journals/alcalc/about.html

- Newsletter: *Alcoholis*
  The bulletin/newsletter of the MCA.
  Published quarterly and distributed to MCA members. It can also be accessed by other interested parties *via* the internet: www.m-c-a.org.uk/publications/newsletter

- Website: www.m-c-a.org.uk includes:-
  - Application forms for membership,
  - On-line access to newsletters,
  - A medical students' page,
  - Notices of activities.

MCA ACTIVITIES:

- **The Michael Frowen Memorial Prize Essay Competition.**

  An annual competition open to all medical students in the UK. There are three monetary prizes which are presented at the MCA Annual General Meeting. The essay awarded first prize will be published in the MCA Annual Report. The first prize winner is also encouraged and supported to publish their essay in a peer–review journal.

- **National Alcohol Awareness Day**

  A competition held in alternative years. The four prize winners are given the opportunity of spending up to three weeks in a well-known addiction centre. Previous winners have visited: Scotland, Vienna, Montreal and Seattle.

- **Seminars/Lectures**

  The MCA contributes to seminars or lectures for medical students and other health-care professionals on a number of alcohol-related topics.

- **Enquiry Service**

  The MCA office is always prepared to take enquiries from the public on alcohol issues. Similarly the office responds to enquiries from the media on health issues relating to alcohol.